Drawing the Line

Drawing the Line

CREATIVE WRITING THROUGH THE VISUAL AND PERFORMING ARTS

Barry Gilmore

Calendar Islands Publishers
Portland, Maine

Calendar Islands Publishers LLC
477 Congress Street, Portland, Maine 04101

First Published by Calendar Islands Publishers, 1999
Copyright © 1999 by Barry Gilmore

ISBN 0–9663233–8–6

Library of Congress Cataloging-in-Publication Data
Gilmore, Barry.
    Drawing the line : creative writing through the visual and performing arts / by Barry Gilmore.
        p.   cm.
    "A guide to resources on the internet": p.
    ISBN 0–9663233–8–6   `
    1. Creative writing (Secondary education)   2. Performing arts—Study and teaching (Secondary)   3. Art—Study and teaching (Secondary)   I. Title.
    LB1631.G43   1999
    808'.042'0712—dc21   99–19387
                                                    CIP

Book design by Phillip Augusta

Printed in the United States of America
Docutech T & C 2005

For my wife, Susanna

Contents

Acknowledgments

The idea for this book was suggested to me over a particularly memorable dessert of bread pudding at Pearl's Restaurant in Sewanee, Tennessee. At the risk of overlooking the bread pudding, first thanks for the idea and for helping to turn it into a reality ought to go to my friend and editor, Peter Stillman.

Sue Gilmore and Elisabeth Perry read outlines and drafts and offered good advice. Jennifer Watkins and Andrew Bales contributed ideas, suggestions, and support. The many classroom teachers who allowed me to work with their students, especially Nancy Finney and Pat Albee, deserve more appreciation than I can offer here; I hope that reading their students' work in print will serve as reward enough. The opportunities offered by the Memphis Arts Council's Center for Arts Education were likewise invaluable to me; the teaching artists from whom I've learned and gathered ideas are too numerous to name here, but two, Gregg Hansen and Richard Graham, must be credited for several of the musical activities I've included. Thanks also to the administrators of the Center for Arts Education, including Amelia Barton, Tracey Zerwig Ford, Kay Ross, and Anne Davey. All of the students whose names appear here, as well as the many others who participated in my activities, have my appreciation and my respect.

Introduction

Most writers and writing teachers I've met have, at some time, used a work of art such as a painting, photograph, song, or play as a source of inspiration. There's a lot of value for writers in such works. They contain stories, themes, messages, and characters that writers can draw upon for ideas.

But most of the writers I've known use the arts as a source of inspiration merely by responding to a work as an audience member. This book approaches the arts slightly differently; it explores the *process* of the artist as well as the *product*.

This is a book about writing, and the activities in it are all designed to inspire better student writing. They are divided into four sections: Visual Arts; Music; Acting and Performance; and Folk Art and Craft. The activities are designed to be used in sixth- through twelfth-grade classes, but they could be adapted to any grade level. You don't have to have experience with these art forms in order to engage your class in the activities described here. A willingness to explore and accept challenges will serve as well as any amount of prior knowledge about the visual and performing arts.

Within each of these sections, you'll find individual units that focus on just one element of the artistic process. This is where you'll find the difference between simply writing about a piece of art and writing from the point of view of the artist. I believe that artists, whether they create through paint, movement, sound, or words, share certain basic approaches to the act of creation. All rely on physical stimuli and experience, all embrace common themes in their work, and all look for tools of artistic composition, ways of putting pieces together to create a pleasing and meaningful whole. By examining the tools painters, musicians, dancers, and actors use for artistic composition, writers can enhance their own skill at creating compositions in words.

Here's how each unit is put together: First, there's a section that introduces the topic. Remember that these topics, while they involve the arts, are mainly topics for *writing;* at all times the focus of the lesson should be on how writers can use the arts. This section of each unit might suggest some warm-up activities, but it's mainly to introduce you, the teacher, to a part of the artistic process that will be used for writing ideas.

Next, you'll find an artistic activity. You may wish to substitute activities or abbreviate those described here. That's fine. It's the element of creativity that's important, not the specific exercise.

After the artistic activity, you'll usually find a few questions or suggestions for assignments to get your class started writing. I've tried to put sentences in italics that are worded as I might say them to a class. Don't feel you have to read these sections word for word; they're just suggestions.

You'll also find at least one model poem or story in each section. Again, you can substitute models if you wish, but feel free to share those I've included with your class. The models are mostly by students, with a few works by teachers and myself thrown in. They weren't chosen because they're the greatest pieces I've ever read; rather, I chose solid works by real students that I felt illustrated the point of each assignment nicely.

Finally, you'll find some follow-up activities at the end of each unit. These might be used with your whole class, or they might be offered to individual students who are interested in further investigation of a particular topic.

By focusing on just one element of an art form at a time, your students will learn to apply valuable artistic methods to their writing and will also gain a greater understanding of the art forms included in the book. Rather than simply responding to an artwork emotionally, your class can consider how and why a work was created.

Furthermore, because each unit focuses on a technique rather than an individual artwork, you'll be able to involve students in the exercises through whatever works are available and of interest to you and your students. Writing assignments in the chapter on visual art, for example, always suggest a well-known piece as a starting point for the teacher, but they will be just as effective if used with a trip to the local art museum or even with works from an art class in your school. Don't feel limited to works suggested in these pages; you should use the materials that are available to you through your school library, books you and your students gather, and the Internet resources suggested in the appendix of this book.

THE ARTS AND THE WRITING CLASSROOM

While I was writing this book, I worked as a visiting artist, or what's called a *teaching artist,* in Memphis, Tennessee. I visited classrooms comprised of students of many different backgrounds, ability levels, and ages (from kindergarten through adults). I taught creative writing, mainly, but I also worked on units that involved visual art, dance, drama, music, and general creativity. I worked with hundreds of teachers, thousands of students, and many other artists.

Through all of that work, I came up with only one definitive rule about teaching the arts: *process is everything.* I've met teaching artists who are so sure that the process of art is more important than the product that they seem to feel it's somehow wrong to actually perform or present art. On the other hand, I've also known a lot of teachers who think that their students haven't accomplished a goal if there isn't a high-quality product—a painting, poem, or song—to show at the end of a lesson.

There's a balance, of course. When I say *process is everything,* I don't mean that students shouldn't aim for highly polished, presentable results. Especially in creative writing, it's important that students remember that there is an audience for their work, and that writers who just write for themselves don't usually produce words other people want to hear, anyway.

But how do you get a student to create poems and stories that other people *do* want to hear? The answer is that an arts teacher must instill a sense of the value of the artistic process, not just the product. When a student leaves the classroom, he or she shouldn't take away only a portfolio of work. That student must also leave with the feeling that producing more art will be not just possible but enjoyable. Teaching process is the key to giving a student a love for the arts.

What do I mean, then, when I talk about *process?* The first step to understanding the artistic process is understanding that students must think of art not as an object or a performance only, but as a series of stages with important guidelines to follow at each stage. Here are a few of the guidelines I use in my own classroom:

- *There's no room for negative judgement in the initial act of creation.* Of course, we all make small judgements with every word, brush stroke, or musical note we use. But in general, the first draft of any artwork shouldn't be criticized or disparaged. It's far more important to get the ideas into some form that a student can work with than to shape those ideas perfectly the first time around.

- *Art is always an ongoing series of revisions.* It would be nice if we never had to stop revising, but that's not really practical. Whether you're talking about a story, song, dance, play, or painting, it's important that the artist have more than one chance to get it "right."

- *Art isn't an individual activity; the community is important.* This is true even for the artists (I include writers in that category) who create in total isolation. At some point, the art they create requires an audience, with common perceptions and ideas. For the student, community is even more important. Writers rely on other writers for inspiration, encouragement, and helpful criticism. This means students must read other writers, share their own words, and involve themselves in writing activities with other people.

- *The teacher doesn't know everything.* It's important for students to understand that there are no experts in the act of artistic creation. Everyone experiments, everyone fails, everyone succeeds. That's especially relevant to this book, which may ask you to try out forms of art you've never experienced before. Don't be afraid to look silly in front of your students.

- *Evaluation should be based on effort as much as (or more than) on product.* Classroom teachers must have some guidelines by which to grade. Grading creative work, however, should not be linked either to a sheer number of words or to the "quality" of those words. Rather, grade your students based on the genuine effort put into each piece or an entire portfolio. Evaluate your students based on participation, revision, and the number of assignments attempted. Don't grade drafts or mark down for grammatical and spelling errors that can be corrected in revision.

- *Form and style come one step at a time.* Beginning writers often try to use rhyme, meter, alliteration, symbolism, and every other literary tool all at once. The resulting poems sound more like they were written by amateurs than they have to. Encourage your students to focus on one aspect of the craft at a time. Rhyme and meter should be left alone until your students have experimented with description and imagination in language.

- *Subject matter should focus on the personal.* This is not at all a hard-and-fast rule, but in general, beginning writing (and other art) will be more original and interesting if its subject matter includes details from the artist's own life and experience. Science fiction, horror, and romance stories are rarely involving if they're not written by someone who has experimented with simpler, more personal topics first.

- *Every work has value.* There's no room in the arts classroom for comments like "This is no good," or "This piece really stinks." Have your students save everything, display their visual creations, and reflect on the process itself—how they feel about what they created and why.

- *No rules are absolute.* Every classroom ought to have guidelines, but rules can and should be broken *when doing so is part of creating a better work of art.* That means that a student shouldn't be forced to do an assignment if there's some more pressing artistic work he or she wishes to create.

If you follow these guidelines in your own classroom, you'll find that your students pick up on the idea that a work is important from the moment it is conceived until the moment it is presented to an audience. Art isn't just what you stick on the bulletin board for other people to see; it's the ongoing method of coming up with an idea, putting it into an initial shape, polishing it and revising it until it exists in its most aesthetically pleasing and meaningful form, and then presenting it to others.

You might even find that some students downplay the importance of a finished work and spend most of their time starting projects they don't finish. To combat that tendency, set aside some time at the end of each week or unit to prepare work to be displayed, published, entered in a contest, or otherwise shared with an audience.

An Outline for Student Writing

In this book, you'll be asked to apply these guidelines to many different forms of art—painting, drawing, dancing, acting, and music making. At every step, you'll also be asked to apply them to creative writing. What I hope you'll discover is that the process of creative writing is not so different from the process of creating other kinds of art. In fact, every lesson presented in this book was developed from the basic premise that writers have a lot to learn from the process of other artists.

Before delving into those other art forms, however, it might be a good idea to delve into the process you'll use for writing assignments in your classroom. I've found that most writers have different methods and approaches to writing, but that most writing classrooms operate in a fashion very similar to one another. The general outline for a writing lesson that I present below is one I've seen work again and again. That doesn't mean it's the only possible approach to teaching writing, or that it can't be modified or changed to suit the needs of your classroom. In general, however, these steps have helped me help students bring forth solid, interesting, and original writing.

Step One: The Assignment
This book is full of assignments, all of a certain type. They're artistic experiences that I hope will raise issues and themes relevant not just to one kind of art but to all kinds, especially writing. There are, of course, a million other assignments waiting to be found. The best often have to do with exploring childhood and the past, personal situations and relationships, or common experience; the arts do this. Another value of using the arts to inspire writing is that the arts demand that students acknowledge the physical world in their explorations of ideas and feelings. This, in turn, makes it easier to capture physical details in writing.

How you set up an assignment depends on what kind of a teacher, writer, and person you are. In general, I find it helps to be enthusiastic and involved in the assignment, to make it seem like something you're anxious to try yourself. The key word in that sentence is *try*—writing assignments are not meant to strike everyone equally every time. Instead, concentrate on encouraging your students to make an effort with each assignment, accept failures, enjoy successes, and prepare to move on.

As you look through the units in this book, you'll see that the assignments include both activities and suggested topics for writing. The suggested prompts will help students relate the activities and themes they embody to their own lives, and to convert those ideas into words.

Step Two: Modeling

It's not necessary to use a model poem or story with every assignment you present, but it often helps students get started. Furthermore, while you should discourage outright plagiarism of other writers, don't be alarmed if your students produce pieces that are very close to the original model in style or form. Learning any art requires imitation. Just be sure that you stress the need for variation and, eventually, originality, even if the inspiration for a piece is another writer's work.

I like to use models by other students as often as possible. I include works by published writers and even, occasionally, works of literature from great poets of past centuries. Most often, though, I find that students respond best—and imitate best—those pieces that sound and feel closer to them and to the way they use language.

Step Three: Fast-writing

Fast-writing is a method of getting words and ideas down on paper without the intimidation of worrying about whether or not what you're saying is "good." I suggest fast-writing as a way of jumping off of any writing assignment. Here's how I might give instructions for fast-writing to a class:

Take a pencil and a piece of paper and write down everything that comes into your head. Don't worry about grammar, spelling, or punctuation errors; there will be time to fix those later. Also, don't worry about form. Just try to get down as many words as possible. If you get stuck, return to the assignment, reread what you've written, or write about something else entirely, like what you had for breakfast. Just don't stop writing.

As your students grow more proficient at fast-writing and at creative writing in general, you'll find that what emerges from a fast-write is often a shaped piece that needs only a little revision. But you shouldn't be concerned if a fast-write contains errors or seems to meander off topic. After your students have completed a fast-write, have them read over what they've written, circle or underline anything that sounds good or sparks another idea, and then use that word or phrase as a starting point for revision.

A couple of suggestions. First, have your students fast-write as a group. There's something about the intensity of a whole class struggling to capture ideas at the same time that helps every writer in the room. Second, time your fast-writes. Students can always write for a longer period if they want to, but it helps many writers to know that the end is in sight. I suggest ten minutes. Third, don't grade fast-writes. Wait for revisions and polished products to evaluate.

Step Four: Peer Evaluation and Revision

A writer in a writing class has a unique opportunity for peer evaluation. Many professional writers struggle to find good readers; a writing classroom is full of them. Encourage your students to share their work in pairs and groups. Make sure you set up some ground rules. Here are mine: (1) the first thing said must always be positive; (2) everyone must treat each piece as if it were his or her own; and (3) the author of the piece is not allowed to explain or defend the words until he or she has heard other students try to explain them first.

Revision involves reworking fast-writes and drafts into more polished pieces. This is the time to consider mechanical errors and form. I encourage students to type their pieces as often as possible after (or even during) the initial fast-write session. This allows them to see the piece more objectively, it slows them down during the revision process, and, if they use computers, it offers them the chance to try very different forms and line breaks very quickly. Allow your students to decide for themselves, as much as possible, how many revisions to complete before bringing a piece to a peer-evaluation group.

Step Five: Presentation

At some point, you'll want an audience to hear or read the works your students have created; this is a valuable part of the process. Magazines, bulletin boards, gift cards, public readings, and contests all offer opportunities for your students to share what they've created with their peers, parents, and the community in which they live. Final drafts should be presented along with the artwork that inspired them or that they inspired.

This step, along with participation during peer evaluation and efforts at revision, provides the most concrete basis for assessment of creative work. Ask your students to provide you with rough and final drafts, estimates of time spent revising, signatures from peers with whom they shared work, or any other records that will offer you some guidelines for grading without simply assigning a number or letter grade based on how "good" a poem or story is.

Step Six: Starting Over
The writing process never stops. Your students might work on a fast-write, revise an earlier piece, engage in an activity, and read a poem to a group all in the same class period. Be flexible—allow your students to work at different speeds, and don't insist that every student or every piece be at the same stage of development.

One of the fundamental precepts of the artistic process is that there is as much to be learned from the act of creation as from the creation itself. The role of the artist is not just to educate, entertain, and enlighten an audience, but also to help himself or herself learn more along the way. The writing process emphasizes discovery in each stage of creation, not just the first time a word appears upon the page.

A final note: It's my belief that the sort of arts-integrated curriculum presented here will only gain popularity in the future. Standardized testing around the country has begun to rely more and more on writing in reaction to given materials such as pictures and creative situations. Many schools are turning to Howard Gardner's theory of multiple intelligences—which includes the idea that some students learn primarily through musical, kinesthetic, and spatial associations, among others—as a source for developing programs. High schools trying to create multidisciplinary programs turn to the arts and to literature as a way of exploring social studies, science, and other subjects.

It's only natural that writing teachers look to the arts for inspiration; creative writing is, after all, an art itself. The connections are there, they are powerful, and they offer real opportunities for discovery. Not every assignment will reach every student, but every assignment will probably reach *some* student.

The important role for the teacher is to allow the process of creativity to occur. Encourage your students, give them opportunities, allow them failures, appreciate successes. Creative writing is not only about words on the page; it's about thoughts, ideas, feelings, connections, memories, and actions. Have fun exploring these elements of writing, and your students will have fun too. That's the most valuable experience any writing teacher can offer.

Chapter One

Seeing Through the Eyes

T H E   V I S U A L   A R T S

*A*rt is about objects. The visual arts, such as painting and drawing, rely on the physical world and how the artist sees it for their medium and subject matter both. Even the most abstract modern painting may remind us of shapes, places, or experiences that exist in the solid and concrete world around us.

Writing is about objects, too, and every artistic activity in this chapter is designed to provide a link between the process of representing objects in art and real creative writing assignments. Like painters, writers have the ability to craft and change scenery so that these objects take on forms, patterns, or shades that weren't immediately apparent before. Think of this craft like standing in a carnival fun house full of mirrors. Some of the mirrors reflect reality just as we see it, while others distort images and make them wider or skinnier, taller or shorter. *All* of the mirrors, however, depend upon the physical world for the images they reflect. And our reactions to the reflections, whether we laugh or scream, come from our comparison of what we see reflected to reality.

Of course, both art and writing allow us to investigate ideas, abstract theories, and emotions. But imagine that you hold in your hands a paintbrush, palette, and canvas. Your instructions are to paint a picture of one of the following: peace, hatred, envy, love, or joy. Where will you start? At best, you might be able to work back towards an actual image, a heart or a dove or a gun. When you've finished such a painting, how many people will be able to interpret its message? More important, what will it teach them about the large concept you were trying to paint? Everyone knows that peace is symbolized by a dove, but does seeing a dove on the canvas really make us feel peaceful?

Most painters, of course, *don't* start this way. Instead, they choose a scene, an object, or a person, and they begin by painting what they see. If they want, they can then change details, colors, or positions to make a statement, to suggest love or peace or hatred. It's a natural way for an artist to begin.

Unfortunately, this approach doesn't seem to be as natural for writers. Most young or inexperienced writers *do* start by trying to write about the large concepts, the abstractions, the grand ideas. Many teenagers write largely about death, for instance, with which they typically have had little experience. Teenagers also write frequently about love, jealousy, and religion. Sometimes they don't realize that simple description and imagery relates these ideas and feelings in an immediate fashion that abstractions can't.

Here's an exercise you can use to try to convince yourself or your students that writing is more interesting when it's rooted in concrete details. Save some greeting cards, the kind with verse on the inside. Anniversary and wedding cards are especially good. Then cut out or photocopy the verses and distribute them to your students.

Ask a couple of people to read their cards aloud. One thing they'll probably notice, after hearing two or three, is that they all sound basically the same. They use the same tired metaphors (*love is like a flower*), the same words, even the same rhymes (*wife* and *life*, *heart* and *start*, *eyes* and *lies*).

Now ask your students to look at the verses again and, with a pencil, circle every abstract noun or adjective they can find. Have them call these out to you as you list them on the board. Here are a few I gleaned from actual greeting cards: *happiness, contentment, faith, dreams, inspiration, praise, soul, devotion, hopes and fears, caring.* Many of these words appeared in multiple verses from the cards I looked at.

What do these poems teach you? They're sentimental and heartwarming, and that's okay for a greeting card, but they don't give you new insight on the world, challenge your perceptions, or tell you anything about the person who wrote them.

Now read some of the poems in this book, or look at a few of your favorite poems by well-known poets from the past like Robert Frost, William Shakespeare, or Emily Dickinson (one of my favorites to use with this lesson is "Sunlight" by Seamus Heaney). How often do you *see* the words from the list? How often do you *feel* those words because of the place a writer describes or the action the writer portrays?

Leave your list in a visible place and make the words on it "banned" words. Of course, if your students really feel the need to use one of these words, they should. (Seamus Heaney ends his poem with an image that includes the word *love*, but he's earned it by his use of concrete language.) But most of the time, these words just hide the really interesting parts of a poem or story, and your students should avoid them when they can. You may wish to add to the list as time passes.

We often say that we see with our eyes and think with our brains. Seeing *through* the eyes combines the two, so that the eyes become a conduit for images that translate into feelings and thoughts. That's an important order: images first, thoughts and feelings second. It's what good writing, and good art, rely on.

W RITING   THROUGH   THE   E YES

If you have access to the Internet, look at the appendix of this book to find some sites that include copies of great works of art you can use for this assignment. If you don't have access to the Internet, there are still plenty of ways to expose your students to these works. Have your students look at any famous painting that depicts a scene with one or more people in it and fast-write about it. Ask the class to consider the following questions:

What is going on in the picture? What are the characters thinking? What might they say if they could speak?

What might be happening just before or after the moment frozen in the picture?

How would you describe the colors, textures, and shapes in the painting to someone who couldn't see the work itself?

What is the most interesting detail in the piece?

What would you say if you could speak directly to the characters, the painter, or the painting itself?

When your students are ready to write, tell them not to worry about the form of their words, whether they come out as poetry, story, or essay. Ask them, instead, to concentrate on creating a physical connection to the painting itself through the use of description and concrete images.

My favorite painting to use for this introductory writing session is *Guernica,* by Pablo Picasso. You can find this painting pretty easily by looking in an art history text or by using the Internet sites listed in the appendix. As an alternative, I sometimes borrow a few art books from my school library or from an art teacher and allow students to page through and find individual paintings they particularly like.

Read the following poem by a high school student and consider how it captures the actual imagery of Picasso's painting and also makes that imagery personally relevant:

Guernica

"The dead have no color." -Ad Reinhardt

I've seen them, the weeping townspeople
and the tumbling bull, the snarl-toothed horse
and the hand holding a broken sword,
frozen in monochrome-pale stillness,
screaming without sound.
The dead have no color.
I've seen them, all of them,
seen them reaching toward the sky,
groping for answers, seen their
stubby toes, their slack jaws,
their tear-drop eyes.
Picasso, how could you capture that pain
without feeling it,
or is that why you used no color,
is that why you show the dead
in washed and gutted shades
and simple geometry?
Above all, I have seen the two women,
one left, one right, each reaching upward,
one holding her dead baby,
the other holding only air.

-Robert Kull, 11th grade

In this chapter you'll be asked to put your students not just in the place of the characters of paintings, but also in the position of the artist. The simple artistic activities presented here are not intended to produce great works to be hung in museums, but they are meant to start your students thinking about how the artist sees objects in the world and translates that vision into writing.

Black and White

Try this free-association game with your students. Write the words *Black and White* on the chalkboard. Now ask the class to tell you the first things that pop into their minds when they read those words. Have your students call out their answers and list as many of them as you can on the board.

Brainstorming is a good way to get any writing class rolling. For one thing, there are no wrong answers—anything goes. Brainstorming also frees your students to make connections between different ideas and objects, and it lets them pick up on the ideas of the other writers in the class. In this particular exercise, you'll probably get a variety of responses to the simple phrase you wrote down. A recent class of mine yielded some of the following possibilities: *skin color, newspaper print, Oreo cookies, day and night, good and evil, a tile kitchen floor, a leather purse, simplicity, a pencil, a tennis shoe, love and hate, cheapness.*

For most writers, the words *black and white* immediately bring to mind a complicated jumble of ideas and images. For visual artists, however, the colors themselves often represent an elementary or simplified way of seeing the world. Our most rudimentary artistic creations appear in black and white—doodles, sketches, pencil drawings, diagrams.

The following activity combines the simplicity of black-and-white visual art with the complex ideas writers might apply to the colors. Leave your brainstorming list on the board so that your students have plenty of inspiration while they participate.

Black-and-White Collages

Give each student in your class the following materials: two sheets of white paper, two sheets of black construction paper, scissors, and glue. The instructions are simple: *make something.* The result can be two- or three-dimensional, it can be abstract or concrete, it can represent a single idea or many.

Like brainstorming, this activity has no wrong answers. Whatever your students create will be valid and interesting. Allow time for them to share their results, and perhaps for other students to make observations and ask questions.

The student creations will often be visually striking because of the contrast in the two colors of paper. You can enhance the effect by displaying several or all of the pieces together on a wall or table, so that they form many parts of one large black-and-white composition.

When your students are finished with the activity and are ready to write, ask them to consider some of the following questions:

What do the colors black and white mean to you? Do you feel differently about them after making your collage?

What interesting or striking physical objects and details came to mind while you worked on your collage or looked at others?

Is it more difficult or easier to get across an idea using only these two colors?

Tell your students to write whatever they want, but to include some physical description and imagery. They might wish to begin by describing an object or a scene, or by describing the process of cutting and pasting the colors together. Then, if that description leads them to an emotion, a mood, or an idea, they should remember that abstract feelings and thoughts are more powerful when they're connected closely with a concrete image or detail.

In the following poem, one student attempted to capture both the content of her collage and also the form of the artwork. The lines, divided regularly by syllables, imitate the shapes and forms of the paper in her visual art:

Abstract World

Turns
Bends, three dim-
ension-
al things, curves, twists,

One
and its op-
posite.
turns, curves, Nature's

Paste.
Twists, bends, come
together.
Like a warm win-

Ter
night, on a
cold, sum-
mer day. This is

Life.

-Jeni Welzel, 11th grade

Follow-up Activities

1. Find some black-and-white artwork to discuss as a class. Look for pen-and-ink drawings by Rembrandt, Escher, or any other artist and talk about how and why the artist might limit himself or herself to only these tones.

2. If there are any serious artists in your class, have them bring in some of their own pencil, pen-and-ink, or charcoal drawings to share with the other students. Your students can react to each other's artistic talents by writing about another person's artwork, or by illustrating a poem or story someone else has written.

3. Have your students choose some adjectives and nouns to describe the way they feel in various situations. Then ask them to write the words themselves, using only a pencil and a sheet of white typing paper, in such a way that the result illustrates the meaning of the word. For instance, you might draw the letters of the word *anxious* scattered around the page, or the word *exhausted* deflating like a popped balloon. This is a fun activity to do in pairs.

C O L O R

My wife plays the violin. As I write this sentence, she's practicing in another room of our house. I don't know the name of the piece or when it was written, but the music elicits feelings and memories just by its sound. Sometimes the melodies she plays are so evocative that I have to stop whatever I'm doing and just listen.

When Russian-born artist Marc Chagall painted violinists, he made them green. In his works *The Fiddler* and *Green Violinist,* both painted early in this century, Chagall gave his musicians bright green hands and faces. In *Green Violinist* the player also wears a deep purple coat, while behind him are arranged the drab and much smaller scenes of a quaint village, including houses, trees, and an interested dog.

By altering the reality of the scene slightly, Chagall captured what I feel when I listen to my wife play. The green figures in his works become the center of creativity and imagination for whole villages. While the musicians play, nothing else is as interesting or as "colorful" as the music.

Colors resonate with us in ways we don't always understand or even notice. We learn early on to associate colors with emotions: red connotes anger, white suggests purity, red and green together remind us of Christmas. Painters work with this resonance both in choosing the colors with which they paint and also when they combine those colors.

Color Collages

One reason red and green seem bright and cheery at Christmas is that they stand out so boldly. Green and blue, on the other hand, evoke deeper moods and remind us, for example, of the ocean. Artists spend a lot of time thinking about when to use complementary colors (those most distant from one another in the color spectrum) and when to use colors that blend. As writers, we can create more interesting visual imagery if we, too, anticipate the effects colors in our scenes and descriptions will have on the reader's mental picture and emotional reactions.

Ask your students to make a list of colors and the emotions they associate with them. They'll probably give you one simple adjective for each color, such as jealousy for green, evil for black, or cheerfulness for orange.

Then share one or more of these works with your class: *The Artist's Bedroom at Arles* by van Gogh, *The Yellow Cow* by Franz Marc, or *Yellow Christ* by Gauguin (again, these are works readily available in most art history texts or at the Internet sites listed in the appendix). Ask your students to consider how color affects the overall meaning or the impression they get when they look at the paintings. Though you couldn't tell just by viewing the piece, van Gogh's picture of his bedroom at Arles is not an exact reproduction of reality—the artist changed the furniture from white to yellow to make the scene more cheerful and sunny.

The following assignment is much like the collage activity in the last unit, "Black and White." However, since everything in our lives happens in full color, you don't have to limit the artistic subject to an idea involving only two colors. Instead, have your students think of a particular scene or time they would like to portray in a full-color collage.

Lay out stacks of colored construction paper, scissors, and glue. You can also use crayons, markers, or even paint such as watercolors. There is a benefit to limiting the number of colors students can use, since with only a few colors the compositions come out with greater contrast between colors and a greater definition of objects. You might offer a few examples to help them get started. Here are some I often use:

Try to remember a time when you felt particularly happy and safe, but didn't know something scary or dangerous was happening or about to happen.

Picture a room in the house you grew up in that you associate with certain colors or shades.

Think of a favorite article of clothing you owned as a child. What color was it?

Pick an animal you like or feel a connection to. How is this animal usually portrayed? What traits do you associate with it?

Have your students make an artistic representation of one of these ideas (or of another idea involving color). I usually suggest the following:

1. *Don't worry about the "quality" of the art—you are after the ideas, not an exact duplicate of something real.*

2. *Nothing has to be the color it was in reality. Feel free to change the color of any object, but try to do so with an artistic or thematic reason.*

When the collages are finished, give the following instructions for writing:

Rewrite your picture in words. Describe the scene, object, or event for us, including as many colors as you can. Don't worry about stating the emotional importance of the scene outright; let your colors do that for you.

Display the artwork and the written pieces together.

Here's a free-write of this sort by a high school teacher. In this poem, Crystie Ballard uses color to conjure the vividness and freshness of a scene that she feels as if she's seeing "for the first time":

> it's as if I see the ground for the first time
> my feet sinking into the mud
> my eyes swallowing old familiar colors
> browns and greens pressed into the earth
> the saturated colors of the seasons
> soaking up their own exposure
>
> it's as if I sit on this back step for the first time
> staring into the meadow
> sudden glimpses of dash and swoop
> as if it were more inhabited
> as if more than birds were flying there
> I can breathe deeper of the creek now
> of the still green trees that stand
> of the light revealing all of the summer's
> buried treasure
> an old bucket
> a blue frisbee
> a yellow pillow
>
> these are things I haven't seen in awhile
> and it's as if I've never seen them before
> this is why I love the seasons
> the constant surprise when you look out the window
> when you inhale the changing colors
> when you meet the moment unexpected
> as if you've never met it before
>
> *-Crystie Ballard, teacher*

Follow-up Activities

1. Hand out copies of the following eight poems by William Carlos
    Williams, one to each student: "Trees," "The Lonely Street," "The
    Pot of Flowers," "On Gay Wallpaper," "The Yellow Chimney," "Nan-
    tucket," "The Bitter World of Spring," and an excerpt from "The
    Descent of Winter" identified by its date, "10/22." It's okay to use
    each poem more than once; two or three students might receive cop-
    ies of the same poem. Ask the students to read the poems once. Tell
    them not to worry if they don't understand the poem completely.
    Then ask them to read the poems again, and this time to circle any
    word or phrase that includes a color. They may also, if they wish,
    circle any nouns that *suggest* a color, and write a suggested color next
    to the word they circled.

    Williams, who described himself as "a writer, at one time hipped
    on painting," was interested not just in color but also in the way
    colors interact. Many of his poems include several colors, all of which
    together make up a visual scene. The most obvious example is
    Williams' famous poem "The Red Wheelbarrow." Discuss with the
    class what, exactly, "depends" upon the image of the red wheelbarrow
    and white chickens. The usual conclusion is that both that poem and
    poetry itself depend on imagery and physical description of this kind.
    I also like to read "The Great Figure," and show students the paint-
    ing Charles Demuth based on this poem, which he titled *The Figure
    5 in Gold.*

    After the students have read their poems, have them create col-
    lage illustrations of the poems. This time, however, rather than writ-
    ing about their own collages, ask each person to trade finished col-
    lages with someone else, and then to write a poem or story based on
    someone else's work. I like this activity because it provides both an
    artistic writing experience and also a chance to share some great po-
    etry with the class.

2. Remember your childhood box of sixty-four crayons? It seemed like
    a lot of colors at the time, especially when you read the names of the
    colors—cornflower blue, burnt sienna, goldenrod. Have your stu-
    dents pick out five of their favorite colors from a box of crayons and
    use the names in a poem. You can also do this with some fancy

clothing catalogs, which include clothing colors such as lake, oatmeal, and thistle.

LIGHT AND SHADOW

Your writing students may not think much about light, but this unit may show them how valuable a tool light can be for a writer. Light informs us about our world. Colors, shapes, and even textures all appear as they do because of the way light reflects off different surfaces. Light also helps determine how we feel. Most people work better in rooms with certain kinds of light, and the lack of light can cause fear, depression, or sleepiness.

Look around the room you're sitting in right now. Where are the light sources? Is anything reflecting light, glittering, or sparkling? Where are the shadows? Would you prefer the lighting to be different, or has the room been arranged so that the lighting is comfortable?

Chiaroscuro

The dramatic effect of lighting was noticed four hundred years ago (if not far earlier) by painters. Caravaggio and Rembrandt, who lived in the early seventeenth century, both used light and shadow to accent the drama and suspense of their subjects. Caravaggio and Rembrandt often looked to real people and scenes in enclosed, everyday spaces for inspiration rather than to grand religious landscapes and classical subjects.

Take a look at any work by one of these men (they're easily found on the Internet at the sites listed in the appendix). Then ask yourself what first draws your eye in these paintings. The answer, usually, will be a face or central object that is illuminated by light coming from somewhere else in the painting, like a spotlight shone upon a dark stage. At the edges of the pictures, the light will fade to darker shades and shadows.

This technique of contrasting light and dark areas is called *chiaroscuro,* from the Italian words for *clear* and *obscure* (or *light* and *dark*). It's part of what makes some paintings seem so realistic, since it gives a feeling of depth and dimension to the subjects. But in another way, it makes the painting seem like an event taken from the stage, where the light is positioned precisely to heighten the tense emotions and the suspense.

Since Rembrandt's time, artists have used light and shadow in many ways. Edward Hopper's famous painting *Night Cafe* uses light almost as Caravaggio would have. The picture could easily be translated into a stage set for a play, with light spilling from the cafe interior into the city night. But Hopper's painting suggests a different mood from the works of much earlier artists; the spot of light in the midst of darkness here imparts a sense of isolation even in the city, of moodiness and melancholy.

Experimenting with Light and Shadow

For this activity, use a room that can be completely darkened. Cover your windows with dark paper or find a room without windows.

The activity is simple. First, gather several different sources of light: a candle, a lamp, a flashlight, a match, a bare light bulb—anything you can think of that might change the quality, direction, or intensity of the light in the room.

Next, divide your students into small groups. Give each group a different means of producing light and the following instructions:

Create a frozen scene using your light source and the people in your group, as if you were the subject of a painting. Think about where the scene takes place, where the light will be, and what it will illuminate most.

When your students are ready, have them present their tableaux to the rest of the class.

If you want to suggest subjects for the students to use in creating these scenes, try writing down a brief description of a scene in a painting that uses light and shadow. After the students present their scenes, you can compare the results to the actual paintings.

Discuss the tableaux created by the students with the rest of the class. Was the use of lighting effective? Did the scene include any interesting shadows or dark spots? Was anyone intentionally left out of the light? What would happen if you used a different source of light? (Try substituting means of lighting to find out.)

After you've experimented and discussed the various lighting possibilities, prepare your students to write by asking them to consider these questions:

How would you describe any one of these scenes? How would you transfer the mood of the lights and shadows from a visual effect into a verbal one?

Can you remember a time when you felt fear, sadness, or happiness partly (or entirely) because of the presence or absence of light?

Have your students write a poem or story in which light and shadow form a backdrop, create a mood, or change the meaning of someone's actions or words. In this example, Ellen Hock remembered a childhood moment when she tried to re-create an imaginary light. Notice the many sources of light in her poem:

Fairy Circle

There was a circle of green, green grass
between the hills behind my house.
I wove sweet-smelling clover into jewelry.
I wore costumes.
I danced as I imagined fairies do.
I was convinced
they danced in my yard at night,
linking hands in a glowing ring.

On the Fourth of July,
I spun with streaking sparklers
arms spread wide
round and round in my circle
until I stumbled,
fell to the ground,
and watched the sky turn.
Finally, I rose,
reluctant to move homeward.
At the crest of the hill,
I looked back, hoping to catch fairies
twirling in the moon's light.

-Ellen Hock, 11th grade

Follow-up Activities

1. Have your students pay particular attention to how various kinds of light and shadow make them feel as they go about their daily

routines. Have them share their observations with the class and then ask them to write about one particular instance from their notes. The result might be as simple as a physical description of a scene in which lighting plays a role, or it might involve light's effect on their emotions, memories, or ideas.

2. Shine a flashlight or an empty slide projector on a wall and let your students make shadows with their fingers, bodies, or other objects. They'll probably remember doing this from their child-hood—two-fingered rabbits are always a favorite. Ask them to think about their shadows, and whether they've ever tried to out-run or elude their own shadows (if no one mentions him, you might bring up Peter Pan). Then have the class write poems or letters to or about their own shadows. After you complete this exercise, take a look at the painting *Shadow of Death,* by William Holman Hunt.

PERSPECTIVE

Ask children to draw you a picture of the street where they live, and they'll probably produce a row of neat, identical houses, all seen directly from the front. In reality, we usually see streets at angles, with slanting lines, shadows, and obscured views. But *that's* much more difficult to draw, especially without a fair amount of training.

Artists work hard to create perspective in their pictures. Sometimes this means meticulous planning so that objects in the distant background come out at the right size relative to objects in the foreground. Sometimes it means altering the size of certain people or objects to make them more noticeable or important, even if that results in altering reality.

Writers use perspective, too, and though the way we see things sometimes differs from the way visual artists see, perspective in writing is just as important. Every reader needs a vantage point, a direction from which to watch whatever is going on. That's one reason abstractions are dangerous for writers—they rob readers of their connection to the story, and remove the sense of "being there" in a poem or story that comes from concrete description.

The Vanishing Point

When you look at a painting in an art museum, all you're really seeing is a flat piece of canvas with colors on it. Even though your mind is aware of this, your eye tricks you into seeing more—depth and distance in three dimensions.

There are several tricks artists use to create this illusion. One is the strategic placement of shadows, and another is painting a scene so that viewers feel they are looking through a window or doorway. Both of these techniques give us perspective, and they are especially useful for painting indoor scenes.

Artists also create perspective by paying close attention to the size of things and where they are placed. Take a look, for instance, at Leonardo da Vinci's *The Last Supper*. Find the point at which objects in the painting look farthest away (it's the spot in the middle of the picture right above Christ's head). This spot is called a "vanishing point," and da Vinci used it to organize the rest of the picture. Any straight lines, such as the beams of the ceiling or the lines created by the apostles' arms and hands, also direct attention to the vanishing point. More important, the vanishing point gave the artist a tool for making all the objects in the scene seem like they're the right size.

Have your students try drawing a few sketches using a vanishing point; if they want, they can draw lines radiating from the center of the paper to the corners and edges and line objects up along the lines. Even if they only draw stick figures, they'll see the effect.

This simple exercise may be enough to evoke thoughts about where to start writing. A physical description of a scene that includes a horizon and distant objects might make a nice introduction to a story, for instance.

You might also ask your class to consider this question:

A physical vanishing point is the spot in a scene where things become too distant to be seen. Can you think of any other "vanishing points"? Are there places in your life where things become too distant to be seen—physically, emotionally, or mentally?

For writers, perspective takes on a different set of rules. Unlike visual artists, we're not confined to those objects and places that disappear literally before our eyes. We can focus our thinking on distance not just in terms of the physical but also in regard to those things that we remember and with which we feel comfortable.

Isn't there a sort of mental "vanishing point," a spot at which memories become too distant to recall clearly? Or, perhaps, a point at which experiences are just too remote for us to "see" in focus, such as when we try to understand foreign cultures or beliefs? Writers can use perspective in geography, in time, and in familiarity to create links between the physical world and our own thoughts and sensibilities.

I wrote the following poem in the spring of my senior year of college. I was leaving Vermont for good, and found myself thinking of both the past and the future. I also recalled another trick an artist had shared with me for creating perspective: some objects, like mountains, look more and more blue as they get farther away. This poem combines the frequent use of one color with the idea that perspective in time and geography are similar:

The Distance of Things

Distance blues things, the way down on Lake Dunmore,
    now the season's in, two old men
are putting out docks, fixing thick beams in shallow water,
    and beyond them the ridges are tinged
with remote lavender. Though the sounds are softer

from this rock a hundred yards above the shore,
    I can hear the whine of handsaws,
the insistent hammers. In May, when I'm gone,
    they'll hop their two-oar boat out deep, toss
their lines into water, wait for bites. Just now the stone

carries up echoes. I hear snatches of their talk:
    a soft winter, little ice. And suddenly I know
that when I leave this place for the last time
    it too will grow blue as it recedes, although
it will be the thin edge of sand against water, the grey-lime

color of granite turning periwinkle, each thin leaf and stalk
    fading to cornflower blue. I can't say for sure
that in the end all's fringed with lilac,
    but what I remember is in shades of blue—blurred,
watery faces of blue-eyed friends, green-blue grass out back

at my parents' house–and I wonder if when I grow old
　　I'll spend chill March days hauling out docks,
and if I'll view the world in shades dull as old type
　　or blues crisp as ripe berries, deep as shocks
of violets, full and absolute and sharp

as a blue-green planet hurtled around the sun against a cold,
　　black backdrop. Perhaps the colors I see
will not be grays and shadows of people and places gone
　　but instead the spring-sky hue, the free
water-lapping color, the thin, steely sheen of things to be done.

　　-B.G.

Have your students write poems or stories in which they describe objects or a scene that moves from the background to the foreground in two of the following: time, geography, familiarity. If you like, have them list some memories and ideas from their own lives in columns under each of these categories: memories they've almost forgotten, places where they've had a view to the horizon, and times when they felt uncomfortable or surrounded by unfamiliar things. When they write, remind them to include a physical description of some landscape, object, person, or action to ground the poem and give the reader a "point of view."

It might be interesting, once the writing is finished, to try to illustrate what's been written, keeping objects in visual perspective as you do so.

Follow-up Activities

1. Pablo Picasso often painted scenes in which distinct figures and objects could be clearly seen, but that didn't use shadows, a vanishing point, or changing colors to create perspective. Instead, Picasso used overlapping blocks of color and shapes to suggest possibilities to the eye. In some ways, these works are like cartoons, where things don't have to exist in three dimensions to seem real.

    Look at Picasso's *Three Musicians* and see if you can figure out why, when we look at this painting, we see a room with three people and a dog instead of just a bunch of colors. Try covering up different parts of the painting to see if you could still tell what the subject is. Then ask your students to add perspective to the painting using words—have them find a point of view, imagining that they are looking at the scene or are in the scene, and describe what is happening physically from that perspective.

2.   In many paintings, especially those dating from the Middle Ages, perspective is intentionally distorted. Important figures are made very large, while less important objects are made small. Thus, a castle might be smaller than a human being, or a horse smaller than its rider. Find a few very early paintings and look at the artist's use (or neglect) of perspective. Then have each student write a piece in which the space devoted to the description of an object does not reflect the size of the object. Give small objects lots of attention.

COMPOSITION

We use the word *composition* to refer to many different forms of art—writing, music, painting. It's a pretty simple word; if we define it by combining its two Latin roots, it means "putting together." So the composition of an artwork is simply the way its many parts have been put together to form a whole, whether those parts include words, musical notes, or shapes and colors. Your writing students may have been assigned "compositions," but in this unit they should actually learn to *compose* in words.

A painter who sits down to plan the composition of a new work has to consider factors such as the size of objects, their shapes, the number and placement of light and dark areas, colors, and the way lines and angles draw the eye. It's a lot to think about, but at the same time, all of these elements are really just part of the same aspect of the picture—its balance. While riding a bike you've used your physical balance to distribute your weight and force evenly. Balance in a painting isn't all that different. The artist tries to distribute objects and shades so that the meaning is clear and the painting is aesthetically pleasing.

Using a Viewfinder

You'd never take a photograph without looking through the camera first to choose what to include in the frame. Visual art relies on the artist to observe the world and choose a scene to depict. Your class can experience the act of choosing a subject by making a simple viewfinder, a portable window to isolate parts of the world.

To make a viewfinder, simply take a square of cardboard and cut a rectangular opening in the center. The opening should be roughly in a ratio of 3:4, or three inches tall for every four inches wide. You can vary the size by making multiple viewfinders, from 1 $^1/_2$" x 2" to 9" x 12" to 30" x 40" or larger.

Have your students use viewfinders to choose subjects that might be interesting to paint, even if you don't actually plan to paint them. Try looking for scenes in your classroom, in other parts of the school, and outside. Your students can sketch or even write down a description of the best frames, including some notes on the balance of objects, colors, shapes, and patterns.

Of course, the difference between a painting and a photograph is that you can change things in a painting. You might try setting up a few objects on a table and looking at them through the viewfinder, then rearranging them and looking again. Has the scene changed? Does it have more meaning or emotional impact one way than the other?

After your students have shared the results of their experiments with viewfinders, ask them to consider the following questions:

What was the most interesting scene you captured in your viewfinder and why? If you were an artist, would you change that scene at all? How?

If you could use a viewfinder on your own life to freeze a scene and then change things around, how would you use it?

What aspects of your life do you "balance" against one another? Think, for instance, of how you work to balance your time, your friends, your family, your schoolwork, or your emotional states.

When your students are ready, ask them to write a physical description of a scene or an image, paying attention to its "composition." The subject might be one of the scenes they captured with the viewfinder, or it might be a scene from their memory in which different things had to be balanced.

Susan Eringer described the scene in the following excerpt gradually, a piece at a time. First she created an entire composition, and then, eventually, she narrowed her "viewfinder" and ended the piece by freezing one particular image:

> The land my father's father owned spread over a hundred acres of Southern Kentucky. It was dotted with streams, hills, thickets, and dirt roads, but what I remember best is a hollow just off one of the roads where my grandfather took me sometimes. His quiet place, he called it, and sitting on a stone looking out over the depression in the middle of the forest I could see why. Perhaps a stone's throw across, the hollow was far enough from any road that no cars could be heard, and only rarely did a rabbit or bird invade the peaceful space. Sometimes wind knocked through the trees like a fist, or rain pattered against the stone like tiny feet, but these are not really noises, not in the way that a noise breaks silence or a sound disturbs peace.
>
> A few weeks after my grandfather died I walked out to that spot and found, on the ground by the stone where we always sat, a single pine cone. I held it up to the light, traced its ridges with my finger. My father's father was like that: tough, spiny, easily overlooked. I sat with the pine cone on the rock and stayed silent.
>
> *-Susan Eringer, 10th grade*

Follow-up Activities

1. The most famous painting by the French pointillist Georges Seurat is called *Sunday Afternoon on the Island of La Grande Jatte.* To create this painting, Seurat used tiny dots of paint applied to an entire canvas nearly ten feet wide.

   Seurat's painting shows two very distinct patterns of organization. First, the people in the painting and the trees make more or less vertical lines from one side to the other. Second, there is a *Z* shape formed by the shadows and shoreline that softens the effect of these vertical lines.

   Seurat made many practice sketches and paintings of this scene before settling to work on the final product. He isolated certain figures and concentrated on them to get them just right before committing himself to a particular depiction. Take a look at a few of these sketches (you can find some of them by checking the Internet site for the Art Institute of Chicago) and at the finished work with your class, and discuss the ways Seurat planned his composition. Do you think he made the right decisions?

After your discussion, have your students use a viewfinder on the painting to choose one person. Ask them to consider what that person might be thinking or saying. What is the character doing in the park? Have each student write a poem, story, or monologue from the point of view of one particular figure.

When you're finished, you might want to watch or listen to *Sunday in the Park with George*, the musical by Stephen Sondheim. It's based on this painting.

2. Take any poem (especially a very long one) or a novel, and have your students use a "mental" viewfinder on that work. Can they find one scene or image that stands out? Would that image be as effective if taken out of the context of the whole piece?

    Have your students copy the short passage they've isolated, and then give it to someone else in the class. The second student can then write a response to the passage, or continue writing where the passage leaves off.

3. W. H. Auden and William Carlos Williams both wrote poems about a single painting by Pieter Breughel called *The Fall of Icarus.* Both poets are struck by the painting's composition, which depicts Icarus falling while a distant ploughman seems more concerned with his work than the fantastic event in the sky. Look at this work and then read the poems—Auden's is called "Musee des Beaux Arts," and Williams' is one of a series called "Pictures from Breughel." Williams wrote poems reacting to the composition of several other paintings by Breughel, as well. Show a couple of these artworks to your class, including *The Peasant Wedding* and *Hunters in the Snow,* and have them write about the composition. What is the main event? What else is going on? Where is the balance?

THE BRUSH

Means and methods of applying paint to canvas have been changing and adapting for centuries, as artists try to figure out new ways to challenge our eyes and brains. A visit to any modern art museum is an easy way to see any number of different painting techniques: long and short brush strokes; paints applied thickly or lightly, wet or dry, carefully or in splatters with gestures of the artist's body. Your writing students can learn to play with words the same way that many visual artists have tried playing with paint and brush strokes to inspire fresh, new approaches to art.

It's unfortunate that since such experimentation has led visual art away from depicting exact duplicates of reality, many people feel that "modern" art is not art at all or that it's phony, elitist, unintelligible, or ugly. To explain why anyone would create such stuff and take it seriously we create stereotypes of artists who are pretentious, shallow, brooding, or distanced from the "real" world. Some artists fit those stereotypes, but others, including modern artists, seek new approaches to their craft in order to give us something new to think about, or a different way of thinking about things we take for granted.

Tools and Techniques

If you really want to explore the many different uses of paints, brushes, knives, and palettes, invite an artist or art teacher into your classroom to demonstrate a few different techniques. It's quite interesting to see the same subject painted in several different ways, using different media and tools.

You don't have to be an artist, though, to see how paint has been used and to adopt artists' methods. The writer, of course, has essentially only one tool for writing: the pencil. (Pens, typewriters, and computers are really just pencil substitutes; they produce the same characters more quickly.) I'm not suggesting that you try to write in *exactly* the same way an artist paints, but rather that you think about the impulse to use different techniques and what meaning those techniques contribute to a finished work. After all, it's the meaning of things that we, as writers, have to gain from art.

Here are three techniques, along with works in which you can observe them and some suggestions on how to use them for writing assignments. There are many more schools of art, methods of applying paint, and styles of depiction than I've listed here. These approaches are merely some of those that I've found to be popular with students and that are conducive to writing experiences. You may find other techniques that work for your class. Have your students try one or more of the following exercises.

Impressionism
　　Method: Impressionists apply small dabs of color directly to the canvas; the mixing of these colors takes place in the viewer's eye. To

re-create this artistic experience for your class, have them use magic markers, crayons, or pastels to draw a picture, with two rules: no single mark can be longer than your fingernail, and no two marks of the same color should touch one another (you can be flexible on these rules if you want).

Examples: Works by Monet, Manet, Renoir, Degas, Pissarro, Cassatt

Writing: Have your class try writing poems in which no two parts of speech may follow one another, just as no two marks of the same color touched in the artistic exercise above. The rule applies regardless of punctuation, so if you end a sentence with a noun, the next sentence cannot start with one. This exercise makes students think pretty carefully about varying sentence structure and sometimes creates interesting alternative wordings.

Pointillism

Method: Pointillism is similar to Impressionism, although pointillists use only individual dots of color rather than dabs. The result, to a modern viewer, may look something like a photograph blown up until the individual pixels are visible. Your students can draw this way by making dots with crayons or markers. Another possibility is to use a hole punch to make "dots" out of colored construction paper and glue them down.

Examples: Works by Seurat, Signac

Writing: Write poems that use only words of one syllable. Tell your students to strive to keep the poems simple while using interesting words. Two-syllable words might be allowed if they are broken down into separate syllables by a line break. An example of this technique is the poem by Jillion Harris on the next page.

Action Painting (Splattering and Slurring)

Method: An important point about this technique is that the artist moves while creating the artwork. Paint isn't simply hurled at the canvas, but comes as the natural result of a rhythmic and often ballet-like sequence of movements on the part of the artist. If you want to try this with paints, make sure you've put down lots of newspaper or tarps to catch the flying paint. A simpler exercise might be to play some music while your students draw with crayons. Have them stand and only move in rhythm to the music when they mark the paper.

Examples: Works by Pollock, de Kooning

Writing: A fun way to experiment with "action painting" in words is to have your students clip individual words from magazines. Remember that the distribution of paints on the canvas in action painting is not totally random; artists do pay attention to color and form. So that your words won't be totally random, make sure you have separate piles of nouns, adjectives, verbs, and so forth. Then have a student or students distribute the words on a large piece of poster board by tossing them (again, do this to music if you wish). Remind the artist that he or she can consider the whole work and choose to include more of one part of speech or another. When the words have been distributed, tape them down and display the poster so everyone can see. Ask your students to find patterns of words or images to include in a poem. (You might have them fast-write a few phrases before they start to write.)

Here's a poem by Jillion Harris, who based her work on a Seurat painting. Like the painting, the poem is made up of small parts: one-syllable words, brief images, and short lines.

Sunday Afternoon

Bright green grass
    and bright green trees, too.
Dark shade soaks up
the rays of the hot sun.
Lie down, rest, be calm.
    Peace. Be still.
Take in the heat.
    Gaze at the swift boats
as they swim in blue waves.
Clouds rule from high
    in the sky.
Think. Play. Meet and greet,
    free of stress.

-Jillion Harris, 11th grade

Follow-up Activity

There are many other techniques and methods of painting that you can explore with your students. For instance, *glazing* involves mixing colors on the canvas rather than on the palette. Your students can reproduce this technique verbally by mixing parts of speech: first writing down all the nouns in a poem, then all the verbs, adjectives, adverbs, and so on. *Alla Prima* is a term that means "all at once" and describes a method in which a painting is completed in a single session, without built-up layers. A timed fast-write describing a fleeting moment reflects this technique well. *Impasto* painting is a style in which paint is applied thickly so that the texture of the painting is evident; ask your class to brainstorm a list of words that suggest textures and include them in a story. Feel free to have your students seek out other techniques and create their own assignments based on them; the results can be fun and surprising.

PORTRAITS

There's something compelling about a human face in a work of art. Perhaps it's because our faces provide us with so many tools for communication, or perhaps it's just surprising that although centuries have passed, we retain the same physical attributes, expressions, and emotions on our faces that our ancestors had. For writers, describing the face can be one of the most important parts of developing a character; your students can learn from techniques artists have developed over centuries.

I find self-portraits particularly interesting. Because we don't look at our own faces constantly, those times when we see our reflections are inevitably moments for self-criticism and insight. Students, I've found, are often most truthful about themselves if they're writing about their faces. Here's a simple self-description written by a young girl:

> I am a twelve-year-old African American girl. I have a caramel-colored complexion, with dark brown, almost mahogany, eyes. I have brown hair and in the sun you can see natural sandy brown, almost red, streaks in my hair. I have long brown eyelashes the same color as my hair. Also, I have white blotches on the right side of my face, which look like finger marks. That's my real face.
>
> *-Kortney Simmons, 6th grade*

We surround ourselves with portraits, even if we rarely think about it. Homes often have photographs or drawings of the inhabitants displayed prominently, much as large, painted portraits adorned the walls of the wealthy in the past. Advertisements are filled with faces and bodies; can these be considered portraits? We even carry portraits with us—just look at any dollar bill.

Creating Self-Portraits

I like to use crayons for self-portraits. One reason is that it releases students from worrying about being accurate or being "good at art"; no one takes crayons too seriously. A second reason for using crayons is that the class can discuss colors for a few minutes before beginning. I have the students look at the crayon names first and pick out a few they like, and later I remind them to include the names of these colors in their writing. We also discuss the fact that there used to be a color called "flesh" in every box, but it was taken out. What colors, you might ask, can they now use to produce "flesh"?

Have your students look in a mirror and decide where they'll start drawing. Then have them think for a moment about which colors they'll use. I invite them to change their appearance, to use wild colors, or to add a different background. The results are often funny, attractive, and revealing.

Display the portraits and then give the class the following writing possibilities:

Pick a moment in your life when your face showed some sign that things were changing. You might choose the day you started to come to school, a time when you found out something distressing about your family, or a time when you'd just won something. Then describe your physical self at that moment.

Describe your face as it is now. Be honest. Include information about a physical blemish, a piece of jewelry (if you wear it), your lips, your skin, and your nose.

Write a letter or poem to yourself. Tell yourself what you like about your appearance, what you would like to change, and why.

Here's an excerpt from a story in which the narrator describes himself in the third person:

His Mom always told him he had his grandfather's skin, a milky beige. It's dark enough so that if you look at the side of one of his fingers, you can tell where the front and back of his hand began and ended. His tall brown hair is always combed over in the morning when it is still black from the shower. It grows thick on the top, like uncut grass, and may be known to curl at certain lengths or during long periods of shampoo drought. Slightly pointy eyebrows hover over his brown eyes, which often become dark slits dragged down by large bags filled with sleep he never got. When he takes his glasses off, two definitive red marks appear temporarily where his glasses had parked for most of the day.

-Robbie Quinn, 11th grade

Follow-up Activities

1. Any artist who paints a portrait, whether a self-portrait or one of someone else, has to consider one important question before beginning: How closely should the picture adhere to reality? A photograph captures every blemish and imperfection, but a painting doesn't necessarily have to. The artist has the luxury of positioning models carefully before beginning a work, even if the result is intended to look spontaneous. He or she can also alter physical traits, clothing, and backgrounds to inspire certain reactions by the viewer. Look at some portraits with your class and discuss the artist's interpretation. To what extent does this same phenomenon occur in literature?

2. Ask your students to bring in photographs of themselves, or take a snapshot of each student to use. Supply them with magazines and art supplies and ask them to make collages that demonstrate, artistically, who they are. Then have them write about their own faces and bodies while looking at the collage.

3. Ask your students to bring in family pictures taken (or painted) before they were born. Then, as a class, come up with a list of information that would be interesting to know about the subjects of the pictures. You might include who the people were, what they did, where they came from, and why or how they died. Write verbal portraits of the people in the pictures. What the students don't know about the subjects of the pictures, they can make up.

STILL LIFE, MOVING IMAGE

Stories allow a scene to unfold over time, while a painting displays an entire scene at once, usually as a single frozen moment. Some people assume that art has to be that way. It *can't* move, can it? And a still life is, well, what it sounds like. But for centuries, artists have been experimenting with ways to suggest the passage of time and action in their art.

Movement in Painting

I once saw an ancient Greek mosaic that depicted a battle between Alexander the Great and the Persians. The two armies leaned into each other, horses straining and spears pointed, while behind them came waves of reinforcements.

The strategy of the artist was a common one: to create the sense that the armies are in motion by causing the viewer's eye to see a logical progression of moving figures. Much later, in the twelfth century, the Bayeux Tapestry showed a similar progression, stretching over 230 feet. By forcing us to move our eyes across the work of art, an artist can give us a sense of that action unfolding. It's not movement, but it does create a kind of story.

Later artists tried other ways to develop a sense of movement. In his famous painting *The Starry Night,* van Gogh proved that brush strokes and lines could do what others had tried through composition. His night sky seems to whirl and churn, and the cypresses silhouetted by the stars and moon appear as if they might actually sway and rustle. In other paintings, van Gogh creates fields of moving wheat and flying birds with his thick, flowing streaks of paint.

Another fascinating attempt to capture motion in paint is Marcel Duchamp's *Nude Descending a Staircase, no. 2,* painted in 1912. Duchamp, influenced by cubists like Picasso and Braque, painted overlapping images and lines that suggested a human body moving forward at a blur, like a photograph taken while the subject was moving too fast. No one human figure is identifiable in the painting, but we have the overall impression of a single person walking forward. It isn't just that the eye moves across the canvas; you only have to glance at the painting to have the impression of time and motion.

Still Life

A still life, on the other hand, stops motion completely. We've all seen pictures of fruit and flowers. It's tempting to assume that such paintings are nothing more than an artist's attempt to paint something realistically and accurately. A still life is pretty, the argument might go, but it doesn't really say much, does it?

The answer, of course, depends on the artist and the work. There are plenty of paintings that are only intended to reflect the world, and these offer one source of inspiration for writers. After all, writers also concentrate on re-creating objects and details, and it's worthwhile to pay attention to light, color, texture, and composition.

Some still life paintings do provide us with metaphors and ideas through the simple presentation of objects. The term *still life* doesn't mean "dead," after all, but life frozen in a moment of time. The catch, though, is that we can't really freeze life. A painting allows us to capture a moment more or less permanently, but we know even while viewing a work of art that the flowers on the table or the fruit in the bowl probably don't exist anymore.

Some artists depict this idea subtly by including suggestive items in the picture like stopped bottles (showing us that we can look, but can't partake), or signs of time passing, like clocks or shadows. Others make the point in a more obvious fashion; in Abraham Bosschaert's *Omnia Vanitas*, the artist depicts not just flowers but also an old book, a globe, and a skull. Hans Holbein's *The Ambassadors*, painted in the time of Henry VIII, is littered with objects that tell time—clocks, sundials, instruments to study the stars. Across the bottom of the picture is a slash that at first seems nonsensical, until you look at it at just the right angle and find that it's actually a human skull.

Movement and Still Life in Writing

The logical writing assignment that comes from considering such paintings is simple: have your students write poems or stories that either rely on description, like a still life, or rely on action, like a painting of movement.

Before your students write, however, let them experiment with the artistic process of composing such paintings. First, have them gather objects, including fruit or flowers and everyday items from around your classroom or from their own pockets. Ask the class to arrange these objects on a table in several different ways. Does the scene suggest more meaning one way than another? What if you altered the backdrop or changed the lighting?

When they're ready, have your students write poems or vignettes. While these pieces should not rely on much action or story line to relate their meaning, they should not be abstract either. The idea is to convey an idea or a feeling through physical description and metaphor, not through stating the idea outright. If you like, you can give these works a traditional lyric form, such as a sonnet or villanelle.

In the following excerpt from a short story, the narrator creates a lyric tone, where little action takes place other than the sound of crickets and lights of fireflies, and then provides a sudden burst of narrative:

> Nothing moved, not the porch lights, not the car in the driveway. Even the molecules of the air seemed heavy and still, the heat collecting at Jerry's brow. There was a soft humming of crickets, and then, clearly, she saw the fireflies, flickering in the darkness and disappearing, re-appearing. All else was frozen, though frozen wasn't the word for it, not in this heat, not with the humidity collecting like water in a bowl and pressing against her cheeks. Jerry sighed and thought that perhaps she was imagining the perfumed smell of flowers carried on the still air. The humidity made the air an animal, hanging on her neck and shoulder.
>
> Suddenly the car roared to life, the headlights burst apart the darkness with twin beams of solid light, and Jerry's head swung up. No one was supposed to be here. This wasn't supposed to happen.
>
> She stood, ran to the edge of the porch, and dug the heel of one hand against the railing.
>
> "Who's there?" she shouted.
>
> *-Shannon Thacker, 9th grade*

You might also ask your students to write poems that use motion. First, brainstorm a list of action words and write them on the board. Include both verbs and adverbs. Then ask your students to write a poem in which the needle on the speedometer never dips to a low speed. These poems should include action, movement, and the development of a story without heavy reflection or moralizing; tell your students to let the story speak for itself. The trick here is to keep the language poetic and interesting without slowing the pace.

Follow-up Activities

1. Read the poem "The Moose," by Elizabeth Bishop, with your students. This poem is about a bus, a vehicle with an actual speedometer,

driving through New England. Interestingly, the poem begins in a lyrical mode, even though the bus is moving. When the bus stops completely, the "speedometer needle" of the poem rises, and the tone becomes more narrative. If you like, allow the class to map or draw an artistic version of Bishop's poem. Then have your students write poems in which the speed of the objects in the writing is at odds with the pace of the writing itself.

2. After looking at a few still life paintings, have your students write poems about death. The catch: they are not allowed to mention death, dying, or any hint of actual death in the poem. Instead, they must create a sense of death's inevitability through the objects and scenarios they include with words.

Symbols and Myths

William Holman Hunt's painting *Shadow of Death* depicts a young Christ, his arms outstretched with happiness. On the wall behind him is his shadow, in the shape of a cross.

Some stories are so well-known to us that a single symbol or object can suggest volumes of information. Other stories may be told entirely by the information presented in a painting. We aren't aware, for instance, of any facts about *Mona Lisa* that aren't presented in the painting, but most of us know a great deal about da Vinci's other famous painting, *The Last Supper.* Even without the title, we could probably tell what this work is about from the number and appearance of its characters.

Some paintings fall in between. Botticelli's *The Birth of Venus* contains some familiar figures, but parts of the story may need explanation. The beauty and modesty of the goddess of love, for instance, makes her instantly identifiable, but some viewers may not know why she rides a clamshell. The answer is a part of ancient mythology; Venus was reputed to have sprung from the foam of the sea.

Students hear about symbolism all the time while studying literature, but they don't often think to use it in their own work. Discussing ways in which visual artists use symbols and myths can be an interesting way to open your students to ideas about how to color their own works with allusions and references to stories and symbols.

Myth, Legend, and Religion

Painters often look for their subject matter in familiar stories and history. In such paintings, the context is already established. Artists can assume that viewers will recognize the situation and at the same time appreciate the particular vision and imagination of the artist's unique rendition.

Writers, too, often draw on such sources for inspiration. Sometimes a story is loosely based on myth or legend, but even famous writers occasionally just retell a familiar story in a new way. Many of Shakespeare's plays were based on stories or actual events well-known to his audiences.

Look at a painting such as *The Last Supper* or *The Birth of Venus* with your students, and then discuss the artist's adaptation of a well-known story for the work. What has the artist included from the story? What has he left out? Has anything been changed or added? Does the painting make you feel any differently about the characters and events?

Symbols

Literature and art are full of symbols. Sometimes they suggest a very specific meaning or event, but most of the time symbols are physical objects that denote large, abstract ideas. Write the following words on the board and ask your students for a symbol (a physical item) to represent each: *peace, love, war, courage, healing, hatred, faith.* Some of these words might inspire more than one symbol—faith, for instance, might be represented by a cross, a Star of David, or any number of other signs.

Painters also use objects like these to suggest meanings. Some of them are common to many works of art. For example, each saint has certain items, called *attributes* or *icons,* that he or she carries or stands near in many paintings. These are objects from the story of that saint, and they help viewers identify the figure. St. Catherine stands near a wheel, St. Jerome stands near the lion from whose paw he removed a thorn, and St. Peter carries keys. Likewise, there are royal emblems that suggest certain kings, colors that are suggestive of qualities (the Virgin Mary is often portrayed in blue, a sign of royalty and holiness), and animals that we associate with certain ideas. In the famous tapestry *The Lady and the Unicorn,* it's clear that the unicorn suggests that the lady is pure.

These symbols can be useful for writers. But while writers work hard to evoke themes and meanings through the use of physical objects, they also try to avoid cliches. Cliches can be phrases that we hear so often they almost lose their meaning, such as "sly as a fox" or "quick as a wink," but they may also be simple symbols that are over-used, such as an olive branch or a dove for peace. Most writers would consider these objects too obvious and easily contrived to truly suggest a feeling of peace.

Look back at some of the paintings listed in this section, or find some others with religious and mythological subjects. See if you can identify any symbols and what they stand for.

Writing Through Symbolism

It's interesting to see how others react to symbols, even if they don't know what they mean. Have your class design a symbol—any simple design or figure. It may include elements that suggest meanings or ideas to the students, or it may simply be a few random lines.

Ask your students to wear or carry this symbol in plain sight for a whole day. They should watch carefully for reactions on the part of others. How do they feel while wearing this symbol? How does it make others feel?

After sharing their observations, you might ask students for other examples of symbols that are worn or carried. Nazis, Christians, and sports figures all wear symbols sometimes. How do their purposes differ?

Ask your students to write poems or stories that includes symbolism. The symbols should not be cliches, nor should they be too obvious, but they should also be more than simple objects present only for the story's sake. If your students wish, they can write about the symbol your class created and how they feel about it.

Stars

One morning my father came home wearing a star on his chest,
　　laid out cleanly in the casket with shaven cheeks and cut hair,
his uniform crisp, his hands still. I looked at him like that for a long time
　　and then my sister and I went to wait in the car. It was raining.

That night I sat at my window and stared up at the stars
　　in the sky and wondered how they had anything to do with death.
Or honor. Or victims. But then, my father's star was not one of those.
　　It had five pointed spokes and a silver gleam like the misshapen,

lopsided things children draw in crayon. And a ribbon. It had that, too.

My father's star was one created by people who didn't think of real stars or of constellations and comets and deep, deep space, and who didn't think of the heavens but only of Heaven.

Sitting in my window that night I wondered
which place my father would rather go.

-Jeanine Raymons, 10th grade

Follow-up Activities

1. Have your students try writing a piece with *no* symbols. Other members of the class can read the result and help to rid the writing of any symbolism whatsoever. This may be a good way to get rid of some loaded abstractions in student works.

2. Show some of the following paintings to your class: *The Garden of Delights,* by Hieronymous Bosch; *The Wonders of Nature,* by René Magritte; *The Persistence of Memory,* by Salvador Dalí, or *The Lady and the Unicorn* tapestries. Then ask them to create a myth or legend to explain the subject of the painting.

3. Read some of these poems with your class and discuss the use of symbolism or mythological reference: "The Second Coming," by William Butler Yeats; "Ulysses," by Alfred, Lord Tennyson; "The World Is Too Much With Us," by William Wordsworth; and "[Sometime During Eternity]" by Lawrence Ferlinghetti.

PHOTOGRAPHY

"Steerage"
(based on a photo by Alfred Stieglitz)

Covered heads
shawls or the thick black hats

White dress, black suit
Too hot for the lower deck

A safe trip home
Cover Georgia's canvas
A slight breeze and the mist
Comfortable for the upper deck.

A new life
Home is a chest carried
It is tough
but the ground is soft

America, social and political
Epitomized in a flash
Captured is the lower deck
Explained, unveiled in black and white

The bridge crossing the deck is clear
"Moshe, no, we must wait to dock"
Uncle will be found eventually
Uncle is an ocean behind

Colorless history is summed
The hot lower deck
The chest
The child

Steerage
Steering lives
Steering a boat
Steering a camera

The black and white has memory
Your memory, mine, his
The history
The Uncle
America

-Rachel Bloomekatz, 10th grade

This poem emerged from a fast-write composed by Rachel while she looked at a black-and-white photograph of immigrants arriving in the early part of this century. The description comes from what she saw; the ideas come from what she imagined.

Almost all writers and writing teachers I've known have used photographs to help with their own writing. Photographs have many of the same artistic qualities as paintings and drawing, with an important difference—there's almost never anything added to or taken away from a photograph that didn't exist in reality. Painters can add or remove people, colors, shapes, and scenery, but the photographer works with what is there in front of him or her.

Because of the dependence of photographers on the world as it exists, some visual elements become even more important to an artist using a camera. Composition, light and shadow, perspective, and color are all vitally important to the meaning and message of a photograph. The photographer must make artistic decisions, often in a mere second or two, and often *before* taking the picture, which will determine how the world is seen in each particular frame.

Try starting your unit on photography by having your students react to the content of a photograph, and then move on to the techniques and concerns of photographers themselves. Have the students bring photographs to class—preferably pictures taken before they were born, although especially interesting recent photographs are okay, as well. They can use their own photos or trade with other members of the class.

Each student should write about one picture from the point of view of a person in the picture or of the photographer. They may wish to address the photographer or the picture's subject, or they may wish to write about the scene itself, as Rachel did in her poem. Invite them to be creative and to imagine what the characters might be thinking, saying, or doing, even if they have to make this information up. It's important to remember that although a photograph depicts an event or a scene that actually existed, writers don't have to be bound by the facts.

Thinking Like the Photographer

There is, of course, a physical and chemical process to photography that's fairly interesting. It begins with the exposure of substances to light;

certainly, there's rich material for writing in the idea of "exposure" and what it means in writing and everyday life.

But it's the *artistic* process that photographers use that this activity will explore. To try it out, all you need to do are these two things: think about the art of taking pictures, and, naturally, go out and take a few yourself.

Some of your students may have cameras that they can share, but you might want to buy (or have them bring to class) a few disposable cameras. These are fairly cheap, although you probably won't find one that doesn't use color film. If you want to have your class take black-and-white photos, use your own cameras.

First, look back over the units in this book so far and decide which of the elements of the visual arts you think are important to photographers. I'd suggest using the following five categories: Light and Shadow; Perspective; Composition; Portraits and Still Life; Moving Image. If you want to add Color or Black and White, fine. You can tell students to use all of the categories on this list for this assignment, or you may let them choose just a few.

Write the categories on the board and discuss each one. How will it apply to taking a photograph? What will the person behind the camera lens need to think about? What might be some possible problems, considering the equipment available to you, and how might you overcome them?

Then have each person begin a chart for themselves, with the following headings:

Photography Record

Name:
Date:

Exposure #	Subject	Artistic Concern

As your students take pictures, they should make a few notes for each picture they take. Under the first column, they can write the number of the exposure as it's shown on their camera. In the second column, they will briefly describe what they took a picture of, and under the third column, they will note which element of the creative process they were thinking of when they took the picture.

A finished chart might look like this:

Photography Record

Name: John Shutter
Date: May, 1999

Exposure #	Subject	Artistic Concern
1	Trees and houses	Light and Shadow
2	Mr. Smith	Portrait
3	Me	Self-Portrait
4	Dad's car	Composition, Perspective
5	My sister swinging	Moving Image

You can find film that has twelve, twenty-four, or thirty-six exposures, and you can choose black-and-white or color slides or prints. If the film has twenty-four exposures, then each student might take four or five pictures for each element of the artistic process.

Have the pictures developed (or do it yourself in your school's darkroom) and share the results. Have each student briefly write a response to his or her own work. What worked well? What didn't? How could the pictures be better? What did the student learn? What was the best thing about this process?

Share a few photographs by professionals with your students. As you look at each one, discuss how the artists used the elements on your list to their advantage. Pictures by Ansel Adams, Alfred Stieglitz, Edward Weston, Dorothea Lange, or Diane Arbus should be in books your students can find in the library or on the Internet.

Create a class gallery and display the best photograph from each student. Include written descriptions of the pieces with explanations of the process or subject material. Then, when your students are ready to write, give them the following ideas as starters:

Write a poem or story about one of your pictures. Include some description of the subject using the same process as the photograph—composition or light and shadow, for instance.

The pictures you captured on film portray just one frozen moment of time. Write about what was happening before and after the moment in the picture, or write about the difference between "frozen" time and real time.

Write from your own point of view as the photographer. What were you thinking at the moment you took the photograph? What were your feelings, hopes, concerns, and ideas?

In the following poem, one student tried to transform the effects of light in a photograph into a moment of revelation in words. Remember that sometimes simple description of a scene or image can be a very powerful means of communication.

Wonder

a unique photograph
the blue-green sea lay before me
like a comforting blanket
dark ravening clouds
with shades of gray hovered above the
calm, restful ocean
the most amazing aspect of this world
inside the photograph
was that, in spite of the dreary clouds
gathered about, one beautiful ray of light
rebelliously shot through the dark wall
and shone as a boundless spotlight
cast on the still floor below.

-Laura Wright, 11th grade

Follow-up Activities

1. Photographs are based on what actually exists in nature and the world around us. To re-create this element of the art in writing, have your students write found poems. Found poems are simply writing taken directly from other sources: graffiti, ads, pages of textbooks, newspapers, letters, journals, or any other written material. You might set rules as a class: a number of lines, whether or not words can be added that are not in the original text, how many words must be taken together from the text, and whether or not it's okay to reuse words or phrases.

2. Create a class "poetry camera." This is just a box with phrases of pure description inside: "a yellow dog," or "the white linen bed sheet," for instance. When enough phrases have been collected, remove them from the box and "develop" them into poems.

3. One of the most common uses of photography today is for identification purposes. Take pictures of each student and make them into "poetry passports" by pasting them inside folded, decorated pieces of cardboard. Then have the students write poems or stories about imaginary or real places. Each time they turn in a story or poem, stamp the passport with the name of the destination, length of stay, and other information. This assignment works particularly well with younger students.

SCULPTURE

Look at any tree, rock, or cloud, and your brain might lead you to associate the shape with more than what's actually there. The tree may resemble a human figure, the rock an animal, and the cloud an automobile.

Before a sculptor ever lifts a chisel, shapes a piece of clay, or carves a block of wood, he or she has to think about what the subject of the work will be. This isn't much different from other artists, or even writers, who face the same task before each new work is created. But staring at a blank canvas or sheet of paper in a typewriter is not the same as pondering the possibilities of what might be made from a three-dimensional block of marble, clay, or wood.

Often the subject matter is predetermined; sculptors might have a particular model, a scene they've been commissioned to portray, or a purpose for the sculpture. At other times, however, a sculptor might let the material guide the act of creation.

If a piece of wood reminds an artist of a particular animal, say a bird or a turtle, then why not let the suggestion guide the work of art? A block of granite might suggest the shape of a person lying down, bending, or praying. Of course, this is an oversimplification of the process many artists use, since one point of sculpture is to alter materials to portray other objects or scenes. But it's not a bad idea for any sculptor—or writer—to take some time to consider the natural shape of things.

Here's a way to experiment with your students. First, have each of your class members bring in a natural object, such as a stick, leaf, rock, or tree. (You can use photographs but actual objects are better.) As a class, do a timed fast-write in which each composes a catalog of as many associations as he or she can find based on the shape of the object. This assignment may result first in a simple list, or it might include short phrases, beginnings of poems, paragraphs of description, or story ideas. Everything the student writes, however, should somehow be an idea that is suggested by *shape*.

Some students may wish to refine a part of this fast-write into a more polished piece. Others might need more prompting. For those, give each student a small lump of modeling clay. You can conduct this activity fairly quickly, if you like. Give everyone one minute (or less) to change the shape of one lump of clay. The results should not be finished pieces; in fact, they might be lumps in slightly different shapes than the lumps they started with.

Now have everyone swap lumps. The second student ought to have five minutes to work with the clay, retaining the basic form or shape determined by the first student. The second student can refine, smooth, roughen, and make any other changes that do not fundamentally alter the original shape of the clay.

Share the results and discuss the process. Was it hard to retain the original shape? Did it suggest subject matter you might not have thought of before?

When you're ready to write, you might suggest a couple of ideas. First, some students may wish to describe their artistic creations in words. Others may find a way to use shape in description and metaphor to create a poem or story.

A fun writing assignment is to create shaped (also called "concrete") poems. In these poems, the words should create a visual shape on the page that suggests or enhances the meaning of the text itself. Try having students write these poems in the shape of their clay sculptures. Jeni's poem, shown on the opposite page, is a good example.

Frustration

The balloon
flat and lifeless
smooth, dull, red I
fill it with air, it springs
to life; more air. Once silky,
currently sticky stretching to
its peak. Pulling apart, giving up, pieces of the smooth, flat rubber
scatter.

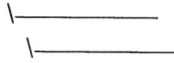

_____

_____

-Jeni Welzel, 11th grade

Follow-up Activities

1. See if your students can find pictures of sculptures by Rodin, Michelangelo, Moore, or Calder. Have them write pieces in response or reaction to a specific piece, such as Rodin's *The Thinker,* concentrating on using physical language and shape.

2. Have your class make sculptures from wire, aluminum foil, Styrofoam, etc. Try making memorials, busts, or turning poems or stories your students have written into sculptures. Write about the process of creating a three-dimensional representation out of raw materials. Garbage and found object sculptures are fun, too; ask students to collect materials from recycling bins at home. These artworks offer yet another aspect of the process to write about—the reuse and rebirth of materials.

3. Your students can play with the process of "sculpting" words out of raw materials. Have one student list up to fifteen or twenty words (interesting words, but not too off-the-wall) on a sheet of paper. Then have a second student "sculpt" these words into shape—perhaps a poem that uses all of the words, plus a few others, in the order in which they were first written down.

Chapter Two

The Mosaic of the Air

*A*lmost everyone enjoys listening to *some* kind of music. You probably have a favorite radio station and sing along with some of the songs when you're alone in your car, or recall them while you're in the shower. It's only when people are asked to make music in public that they turn shy. That's when some people feel that they don't have enough skill to create good music.

The truth is that musicians (and other artists as well) aren't doing anything mysterious or mystical. They're simply putting together small pieces to form a whole work: sounds, beats, energy, emotion. Most important, they're making decisions based on what feels right, and no one else can tell you what feels right for you. That's a little scary, because it means you're the only judge, finally, of what you do, but it's also liberating.

Here are my rules for any group of students involved in making or listening to music:

1. *You're making something with meaning, even if the meaning isn't lofty or even nice. Think about what you want to say with the artistic tools you have.*

2. *There's no place in a classroom for statements such as "This music is awful." People often say this about music that millions of others love. A better response is to figure out what about the music you like, what about the music you don't like, and why.*

3. *Everyone has musical ability. Everyone can participate.*

If you or your students don't accept these statements as true, that doesn't mean you can't learn from and even enjoy music. But it can mean that someone in your classroom won't be experiencing the joy and satisfaction that music offers.

Starting to Listen

The most important skill your writing students can develop in approaching music is listening. Through listening, students can pick up on the many similarities between music and writing and use them to strengthen their own works. Listening is different from hearing. Hearing simply means receiving information in the form of sound waves, the way a calculator receives information when you push the buttons. Listening is about adding that information up, computing it, deciding what it means. Listening involves emotional reactions and the identification of concepts—feeling and thinking.

The good thing about listening is that it's an easy skill to use. Take any piece of music and, after you hear it played, ask yourself the following questions:

What sounds do I hear?
How do those sounds make me feel?
What pictures form in my mind while I listen?

Try this with your class using an unfamiliar piece of music, especially one from a different culture. Try some Chinese opera, African drumming, or Native American flute-playing. After the initial response ("this is weird" or "cool!"), try to identify what you like and dislike about the music and why.

I often perform or play recorded music for classes and have them draw while they listen. This forces the students to think in physical terms, to create metaphors and images for what is essentially an abstract art form. Hearing, I tell the students, is a sense that takes more work than some others, because we're not constantly refining it the way we refine our sense of taste, of feeling, or of sight. So it sometimes helps to work on hearing through the use of the other senses, our memories, and our imagination.

In this poem, Erin Tocknell thought about her sense of hearing while listening to Irish and Appalachian music:

Senses

Most senses come natural as birth
touch of Mama's fingertips
along soft hair line,
eyes adjusting from light
to blurs of color, to shapes
grasped and tasted
creating the need to cry
yell, laugh, sing for ears
that grow less sensitive.

Listening must be honed
sharp as Daddy's pocketknife
but still protected from
the pang of water leaking through the roof,
termites moving in the woodwork,
mongrels fighting in grassless yards.
Children who shut their ears
from the scream of creatures in the hollers
miss cicada choruses in the trees.
Flight from thunder like shotgun blasts
destroys the rhythm of a rainstorm.

Do not close your ears, child
or else they will numb
'til the wind's the same as radio static.
On hillsides, leaves of red and gold
flame in sharp autumn air,
but can you hear them rustle
like Bible pages?

-Erin Tocknell, 12th grade

There's nothing wrong with playing music in the background while you work, humming something without meaning, or not wanting to listen to certain kinds of sounds. But from now on, when you do hear music, whether it's live or recorded, make yourself stop for just a moment and listen. What do you hear? How do you feel about it? Is there anything there that you hadn't noticed before?

If there is, then the music has done its job.

S O U N D

We all know that words use sound, but in this unit your students will learn to think of words as a type of music as well. Why is music so appealing? Ask any two people that question and you're not likely to get the same answer. Ask any group of people, in fact, and you may not get two answers that are alike. When I try to figure it out myself, I always have trouble sifting through the possible reasons why a person might like music: cultural background, personal associations, the science of the ear and sound waves, the desire to create order.

The truth is, no one knows for sure why some notes sound good to us when they're played together and some don't. I suspect it has to do with a combination of factors, ranging from our experience with sound as babies to the way our bodies are constructed.

Whatever the reason, however, just about everyone responds to music and sound instantly and with emotion. Whether it's a sonata by Bach or the noise of a jackhammer in the street, sound has an immediate effect on our mental and emotional states. So it stands to reason that musical poetry and language would contain the same power.

Sound is the most basic element of music. There are others—rhythm, volume, and speed, for instance—but sound is as fundamental to music as color is to paintings. In fact, you can think of sounds as being a lot like colors. Different sounds by themselves, like colors, have emotional resonance and association for us, and combined they can outline much larger stories, ideas, and themes.

That's one reason poets often use rhyme in their work—so that the words will provoke feelings not just by their content but also by their *sound*. Rhyme also helps with organization, just as sound helps musicians organize a song. But rhyme isn't the only kind of sound that's important in language. There's also the music of alliteration, for instance, where words start with the same sounds, like a tongue twister. And sound is important when writers use words that sound like the thing they describe (this is called *onomatopoeia*), as in words like *buzz* or *roar*.

Musicians, in fact, sometimes refer to a "vocabulary" of sounds available to them, much as writers might refer to a vocabulary of words. An instrumental musician (one who doesn't include lyrics) has to choose only from sounds to tell a musical story or get across an idea or feeling.

Pitch and Timbre

There are two ways of identifying any sound: by its *pitch* and its *timbre*. *Pitch* refers to how high or low a sound is, while *timbre* refers to the quality of the sound—whether it's made, for example, by a guitar string or by an elephant.

Of the two, pitch is probably the more important for writers. The timbre of words relies on the person reading them, but since words aren't always read aloud, writers have to trust that their readers have common reactions to words when they read them silently.

Pitch, on the other hand, is directly relevant to spoken *and* written language. Try this experiment, for example:

Say this sentence (even in your head) as a statement: "That's the last slice of bread."

Now say it as a question: "That's the last slice of bread?"

Notice how the sound of the words rises at the end of the question? That's the pitch going up. It tells us that the same words are interrogatory and not just an assertion of fact.

Rhyme

My sample sentence wasn't particularly poetic. But what if we wrote it out like this?

> That's—
> sadly—
> the last
> slice
> of bread.

Not much of a poem, I admit, but it's *more* poetic, isn't it? The line breaks help to add rhythm to the words. But if we really want to make it poetic, how about adding rhyme?

> Roses are red, violets are blue,
> That's the last slice of bread, and the last butter too.

Now there's a rhythm and a rhyme—*red* and *bread*—that makes the line sound musical.

The problem with rhyme in English is that it's not easy to do well. For one thing, English doesn't have the proliferation of vowels that languages like Italian or French have, so there aren't as many choices for rhymes. The result is that poets often fall back on the same tired, over-used rhymes, like *wife* and *life, walk* and *talk, run* and *sun.* This is espe-cially disappointing when a poet lets the *rhyme* determine the *content,* rather than the other way around.

On the other hand, rhyme can make a poem more musical and more enjoyable even when it's not especially noticeable. Go back and read the poem "The Distance of Things," in the unit on Perspective in the last chapter. Did you notice the rhymes the first time around? Can you figure out the rhyme scheme now? I didn't want the rhymes in that poem to distract from its content, so I subdued them in two ways. First of all, I let some of the rhymes be paired over stanzas: *Dunmore* and *shore, talk* and *stalk.* Second, I used off-rhymes, words that sound similar but are not complete rhymes. Some examples from the poem are *softer* and *water, men* and *tinged, sure* and *blurred.*

One way I work on rhyme with students is by having them write sonnets. But instead of just making an assignment that everyone write a sonnet, I have the class pick the end rhymes *first.* I go around the room and ask fourteen people to contribute words in a certain order: the first person chooses any word, the second chooses any word, the third person chooses a rhyme for the first word, and the fourth a rhyme for the second word. We continue until we've fulfilled the rhyme scheme of whatever sonnet form we've chosen.

If I discuss off-rhymes with the class before starting this exercise, the words we come up with are usually pretty interesting. Some rhyming pairs I got last time I tried this exercise included *cherry* and *barely, maple* and *contain, microphone* and *cacophony.* Sure, it's a stretch to say these words rhyme, but then, this is just an exercise. The sonnets are much more interesting, as a rule, than those I'd get if all of the rhymes were exact.

Alliteration, Repetition, and Onomatopoeia

Of course, rhyme isn't the only kind of sound that creates music in lan-guage. The first English poets, in fact, didn't rhyme at all. Instead, they wrote alliterative poems, like the Old English epics *Sir Gawain and the Green Knight* and *Beowulf.* Some modern poets have revived this form. A good example is the poem "Junk," by Richard Wilbur.

In a true Anglo-Saxon alliterative line, the line is broken in half, and each half has two heavy stresses. Either the first three or any three of the four stresses start with the same sound. Here's an example:

My wise words,
>   well heeded,
make sound sense
>   for some, not all.

You can try writing alliterative pieces with your class or you might just include some alliteration in a poem or paragraph to make it more musical. If you do, consider tossing in some repetition of words and phrases to create rhythm and pattern as well. You might even include words that suggest meaning by their sounds.

In the following poem, Crystie Ballard uses alliteration, repetition, and sound to create a playful, dreamlike music in her poem. Notice how she turns phrases inside out, repeats whole words and parts of words (like the *-ing* words in the second stanza), and chooses some vocabulary just because she likes the sound of the words themselves:

I dream kaleidoscopes of life
midnight playmates pinching and prodding me
murky adventures in waterfalls of experience
turned inside out
abstract images mingled with imaginary monsters
faces i don't remember
and memories i can't face
i dream reality into tight braids of color and texture
i toss my head in my sleep
at night my mind is an encyclopedia
upside down and on fire

i dream in the daylight too
of loons and lovers mingling
on the shores of my imagination
lapping up and over me
soaking my mind saturating
my thoughts swimming
through thick possibilities
like pondgrasses that tickle my feet
titillating and tormented both

i dream waves of ways to be
i dream spirals of myself

wrapping galactic arms around me
and whispering sweet nothing in my ear

-Crystie Ballard, teacher

Have your students write musical poems without meter. If you want, have each student write one line of a poem, so that the focus of each student becomes the sound of a single line. Most important, have fun with sound and the music of language.

Follow-up Activities

1. Have your students make lists of all the interesting sounds they heard during the course of a class or a day. Then have them write poems or stories in which they include as many of those sounds as possible.

2. Tell your students to pick a period of time—for example, the time from the moment they left their houses this morning until they got to school, or the time it takes them to walk a dog or to do the dishes—and write a poem or story that takes place during that period of time. Remind them to include every sound they can think of that happened during that period.

3. Find some other rhyming forms, like sestinas, villanelles, pantoums, and limericks. Try asking your class to write in these forms with or without meter. Again, you can have your students choose the rhymes beforehand if you like.

FLUTES, STRINGS, DRUMS, AND HORNS

When I was in high school, I played several instruments very badly. I took piano lessons, guitar lessons, played in the school orchestra, and attempted to teach myself to play everything from the tin whistle to the banjo. I got better at some instruments, like the guitar, by practicing diligently. Others I still play very poorly. Nevertheless, I don't think I'll ever be content to play only the one or two instruments I'm actually good at. For one thing, it's easier to understand different kinds of music if you understand the instruments on which they're played. But my interest goes deeper than that; I simply love the different sounds and styles created by different kinds of instruments. For your writing students, those sounds and styles can offer new ways of putting together words, as well.

Creating Instruments

Before I make any instruments with students, I ask them to engage in a very simple listening exercise. I have them find a spot, preferably outside or by an open window, and for five or ten minutes record every sound they hear by writing down the sound or its source.

When they're done, we share the lists of sounds. Then I ask them to pick out only the *natural* sounds on their lists. The results vary depending on where the class is taking place, but usually there are a few similarities: human voices, birds, wind, rain.

The simplest and most primitive instruments tend to imitate some common natural sound. Whistles and simple flutes imitate birds, or wind whistling through trees and crevices. Drums imitate the weather, crashing waves, heartbeats, or any other rhythmic beat. Even stringed instruments are similar to the sound of the human voice, which is produced by vocal chords that vibrate as strings do.

All sound, of course, is produced by vibration, so the key to creating any instrument lies in understanding what needs to vibrate, and how those vibrations will resonate. I like to tell students we're *creating* rather than *building* instruments (though in fact we often do both) because it suggests that anything can be an instrument. You don't have to carve a violin or stretch a goat skin across a drum frame to play music; you can make rhythms and sounds with almost any object. How much you change the object in order to change the sound is up to you.

Usually, I encourage classes to make several different kinds of instruments, so that the variety of sounds in the eventual ensemble will be more varied. I also like to make simple instruments out of easily available materials. Not only does this mean that students can re-create the instruments again more easily, but it also tends to spark ideas for other instruments they might create.

Here are instructions for creating a few instruments for a class orchestra:

Shakers: You can make simple shakers out of Coke cans, aspirin bottles, gourds, or any other container. Simply fill the container with a handful of dry rice or beans and seal it with a lid or tape. Decorate the outside.

Rainsticks: A more complicated kind of shaker is the *rainstick*. In South America, these instruments are made from a thorny tree; the thorns are removed and stuck back into the hollow wood, which is then filled with stones. I like to use cardboard tubes, especially the kind that fabric stores give away after using the material rolled around them. Take a tube and drill or poke tiny holes all over it. Then stick toothpicks into the holes with glue to hold them. When the glue has dried, break off any protruding toothpick ends. Tape one end of the tube and put in a couple of handfuls of beans, split peas, or unpopped popcorn. Then tape the other end of the tube. When you lift one end of this instrument, the beans will shuffle and fall between the toothpicks, creating the sound of rain.

Water Glass Xylophones: Fill water glasses with water to various heights. Tap on each glass with a pencil or mallet to hear different notes. You can tune the glasses to a scale by adding or removing liquid.

Panpipes: Panpipes are primarily a South American instrument, though they're named for a similar set of pipes played by the Greek mythological figure Pan. You can cut panpipes of different lengths from half-inch-diameter PVC tubing, one end of which you should plug with a half-inch PVC cap.

After you cut a length of the tubing with a handsaw, sand the end to make it smooth and easier to play. Then hold the tube vertically below your mouth and rest the open end just under your lower lip. Blow and tilt until you find the right angle to produce a solid, clear note.

If you want to tune a set of pipes, you'll need one pipe for each note. Here are the lengths for notes in a C major scale:

G	8 $1/4$"	D	5 $3/8$"
A	7 $1/4$"	E	4 $3/4$"
B	6 $3/8$"	F	4 $7/16$"
C	6 $1/8$"		

Blowpipes: One of the most successful instruments I've used with high school trumpeters is also the simplest. Just take large tubes of

PVC pipe, perhaps two inches in diameter. Have students "blow" in one end—really, this means pursing the lips and making a sort of buzzing noise, as horn players do. You'll just get one note, but it's a doozy.

Other Rhythm Instruments: Almost anything can become a rhythm instrument. I sometimes have students make sand blocks (sandpaper and blocks of wood); drums out of milk jugs, oatmeal containers, or water cooler bottles; and strings of bells or beads. Ask your students to create other instruments on their own and bring them to share with the class.

Using the Instruments

Divide your students into duets, trios, quartets, or larger ensembles and provide them with the instruments they created. Let any musicians in your class bring other instruments they can play.

Give each ensemble an assignment and have them create a brief performance using their set of instruments. The goal should not be to compose a piece of music so much as to use the sounds of the instruments to produce an impression, setting, or feeling. For instance, you might have ensembles try to re-create the sounds of a traffic jam, a playground, the rain-forest, a desert, or a jungle to the rest of the class. I've also given each group one stanza of Lewis Carroll's poem "The Jabberwocky" and asked them to re-create the action of the poem using sounds.

Another possibility is to distribute the instruments in roughly the order of an actual orchestra. Divide your instruments so that you can imitate the four families of instruments in a professional orchestra: strings, woodwinds, horns, and percussion. The strings (one-string guitars, for instance) should sit together in a semicircle. Behind them, arrange the woodwinds (panpipes, human whistlers, and flutes). Next come the horns (blowpipes), and finally the percussion (shakers, rainsticks, drums, and xylophones). Choose a student conductor and experiment with tempo (speed), dynamics (volume), and entrances and exits of instruments or sections. You might even compose a class piece.

The results of all of this are likely to be fairly ridiculous, but fun nonetheless. Besides, the point will be made: musicians rely on different sounds, produced by different instruments, to suggest a variety of ideas and emotions.

Have each of your students choose just one instrument and give them one minute to list at least five or ten words that *sound* like the noise that instrument makes. If they can think of real words, that's great, but nonsense words might be fine. For example, a list of words that sound like a shaker might include *ticket, chicken, tse-tse fly, zipper,* and *sip.* Words to describe a drum's sound might include *pound, doom, ruin,* and *soon.*

Then have each student write a poem or descriptive paragraph including some of these sounds. The initial results might naturally lead to nonsense poems. Here, for instance, is one such work written in about two minutes by a seventh grader:

> The ocean swirled
> Starlight twinkled
> Saturn whirled
> Wheels buckled
> The grasses blew
> As the doors flew.
>
> -*Caitlin Carter, 7th grade*

Caitlin's assignment was to use lots of sounds like those of her instrument to describe a performance she'd been in; she chose a dance recital.

After playing the classroom instruments they created, your students might appreciate listening to solo performances by musicians on more professional instruments. Ask one of your students to bring an instrument to class and play a solo piece, or invite a band teacher or local musician in to play while your class writes.

The following poem was written by a student learning to play the violin:

The Instrument

> I finger the perfect neck of the wood with the dazzled
>   enchantment of a disciple.
> Nestled in its grains are swollen notes and melodies,
> Caught upon its glaze are beautiful harmonies,
> All the marvelousness I wish to possess bound within its strings,
> And wound tightly through the scroll are the glories it has seen.

I feel a pulsing soreness in my withered fingertips—
My outlets to the pent-up by-products of being—
So I cast off these sluggish weights with the feathery movements
Of elbows, wrists, and hardened fingers,
And they float to the sky, rejoicing in release.

My eyes shut; I draw the music into my ears to feel the joy
Of the single note, simulating an angelic human voice,
Wavering on perfection and godliness, not needing to decide.
This awe-filled consciousness circles my head, and it becomes
My mesmerizing madness of things I've dreamt to keep.

Then I wake up, joyful, from this flowering satisfaction,
I look down at these ten benefactors of my soul
And see not the chiseled and slender statues of my dream, but
Cut and mauled hands and skin, broken fingers,
Broken keys to the treasure locked inside my instrument.

As the reality dawns on my mind—
Of these joints and bones wrongly intertwining to pervert
        marvelous sounds—
my lungs burst with pressure, but my vocal chords,
Unable to produce noise, like my fingers, remain motionless.

Desperate, I scramble to a corner, thrashing violently at the walls
Trying to escape my childhood nightmare—
The green faced witch who laughs at me,
Threatening me for the beauty I thought I could create.

-Zoe Jarman, 9th grade

Follow-up Activities

1. One of the most frustrating moments for any musician is the in-
    stant in which he or she misses a note. Making mistakes is a part
    of performing, but not one any musician enjoys. Look back at
    Zoe Jarman's poem above, and then have your students write about
    their frustration at not being able to perform on an instrument or
    make it sound as they wish it to. Do the limitations placed on

them by a musical instrument symbolize or suggest any other limitations in life?

2. Have students experiment with combinations of instruments in duets and trios. Then, with your class, decide which instruments' sounds blend and which don't. When your students find a combination that they like, have them write a poem or story that uses the sounds of both instruments, or a dialogue between the two. You might also have two people write poems about the same subject, each using the sounds of a different instrument.

3. Prokofiev's *Peter and the Wolf* is a great piece for introducing students to the sounds of different instruments. Listen to this piece and then ask your students to write poems in the voices of the different characters as played by various instruments. Try to imitate the sounds of the instruments in the words and language each character uses.

4. Listen to music from around the world and pick out the sounds of some traditional instruments such as drums, flutes, or strings. What natural sounds are these instruments trying to imitate? Write pieces that are set in that part of the world (try music from Africa, Asia, Native American regions, or Ireland) and that use the sounds of the instruments that come from that region.

THE SINGING VOICE

I still remember the first time I heard Bobby McFerrin sing. I was listening to the radio with a high school friend and heard him perform a live vocal rendition of the Beatles' song "Blackbird." I was stunned.

The human voice is an amazing tool for music making. I was encouraged to sing as a child—most children are—but I never really thought of the voice as an instrument. It wasn't until I started working with music more seriously that I realized how similar to a musical instrument the human body really is. Our bodies produce vibration and sound waves, form resonating chambers, and offer control of pitch and dynamics just like sophisticated man-made instruments. In fact, most instrument makers would be thrilled if they could consistently achieve the range, diversity, and quality of the voices shared by a choir of humans.

Voices like Bobby McFerrin's are rare; I don't have one. My own voice is a little weak and thin, but I sing anyway. If you look at it positively, voices like *anyone's* are rare. Our bodies are living instruments, and as they grow and change each person develops a unique voice.

The Literary Voice

Like singers, poets and authors each have an individual "voice." Yours isn't necessarily the same voice you use to speak during casual conversation; nor does it include only a particular use of sound. Just as singers make stylistic choices, so do writers.

Discovering a voice is a large part of learning to write. Your students' literary voices depend upon their choice of vocabulary, their use of dialect or accent, their sentence structure, and *how* they say things—confidently, meanly, innocently, or happily, for instance.

Of course, characters may speak in different voices, and even narrators may not have the same voice as you the writer. But at some point, everything a student writes comes out of his or her own head. Most writers, and especially poets, discover a particular voice that works its way into their writing again and again, just as singers tend to stick to one style of singing.

Read the following two poems. They were written within days of each other by two students in the same writing group. Each of the poems is a reaction to the attitude of a close friend, but the voices of the speakers are quite different. In the first poem, the speaker comes across as a caring, tender observer:

To Jane

You spin
round and round
ending your combination with a leap
and a crooked smile.
Just a small performance
between classes.
One of many.
Snapping to a West Side Story song,
spinning on.

What gifts you have!
Singing, dancing, acting, joking.

It's all so easy for you.
But you seem to forget all this
the minute you look in the mirror.
All you see is the outside,
your weight,
your clothes,
your skin.

-Elizabeth Eckstein, 11th grade

Where Elizabeth Eckstein's poem paints a picture in short phrases, sentences with several line breaks, and simple language, the next poem does the opposite. Here Elizabeth Kirkindall writes with a sarcastic and cynical voice:

Your parents are basically fine human beings
And your preppie sister, she's OK
    so I don't understand
    why imaginary toxins flow through your virgin veins
    providing sweet relief from despair you've never felt
    and why you wear the green bandana
    of a nonexistent street gang.
At school you exhibit your anguished manhood
    with a sterile bandage round your unharmed wrist
    to impress your friends
    and make your enemies talk.
You spent eight hundred and seventy-two dollars
    on an electric guitar
    that looks great and gathers dust.
And in a secret whisper you curse your birth
    for depriving you
    of that alluring teenage angst.

-Elizabeth Kirkindall, 11th grade

How do the longer sentences, more expansive vocabulary, and sharp tone of this poem change your feelings about the speaker? Neither of these works is necessarily better or worse than the other. Rather, they're different; the voices of the speakers, and perhaps of the poets themselves, provoke very different responses in the reader.

Ask your students to make a list of various phrases, sentences, or ways of speaking they use during the course of a single day. They should try to distance themselves from their own voices just enough to notice how words sound, what kind of slang they use, whether they use interesting vocabulary words, what sort of accent they have, and any other interesting or quirky qualities they give their own speech.

The next day in class, share the observations. Then ask your students to consider how their speaking voices differ from their literary voices. Have them try out a single writing assignment twice, first in their literary voice and then in the voice they would use to speak to a friend. Are they different? Which produces the better results?

Follow-up Activities

1. Voices are categorized by the range of the singer. A woman with a high voice is a soprano, while a woman with a low voice is called an alto. Men's voices, in order of highest to lowest, might be called tenor, baritone, or bass. Listen to a piece of choral music and see if you can identify the various groups. Then have your students try writing in the voice of a soprano, an alto, a tenor, or a bass. How can they make the sounds of the words reflect the sounds of the vocal part—which words, for example, sound high and piercing like the voice of a soprano, and which sound deep and rumbling like a bass?

2. Have each of your students find one of their old poems or stories with which they weren't completely satisfied. Ask them to rewrite the piece using a different literary voice. How might a different tone, new vocabulary, new sentence structure, or different line breaks change the voice and meaning of the work?

METER AND TIME

Sometimes, when they're lucky, writers capture an interesting rhythm without even thinking about it. Words and phrases flow together in a way that sounds satisfying, even if the piece is not in a strict meter such as the iambic pentameter Shakespeare used. Read this poem by Devon Williamson and listen for any regular rhythms:

Beltane Dance
(Si Bheag, Si Mhor)

And field, wheat, fire
harvest around
maiden lock and crescent brows
skirts aswirl,
fermented air
cool, crisp to breathe
spin, spin, and twirl
fall again
to seize the earth,
relish the soil,
hear in your blood
the pulse of flame,
the root of rhythm
to drive you into music
dancing on the Tor
dulcet, ravishing
flesh—bone—
release of the wind from beating arms

pull it
from the Rowan,
the Druids,
from your clan's
acrid sweat
you have wept
sharp mead
you have drunk
in oak taverns tall
on slanting moors
and cracking seas
Fly.
the bubble in melody
sweeps along
to swallow all
joyously give chant
to heather and yew

what is sound but
vibrations in the throat
of your ear
that peal
into your skull
and whip
your head
about your neck
sharp—twist—spring
wheel yourself
into the beat
captured and spun
with the crowned sky.

-*Devon Williamson, 12th grade*

Now go back and read the poem again, and this time, count the number of stresses in each line of the first stanza. These stresses are also called *feet*, and can include one or several syllables and even more than one word. The first line, for instance, contains three stresses or feet, even though there are four words.

Notice, in fact, how many of the lines in Devon's first stanza have three feet. They give the poem a haunting rhythm that drives the long string of images forward. Although she wasn't counting or even consciously including three feet per line, Devon heard the rhythm of the phrases in her head while she was writing. One reason that she heard the lines this way may be that she wrote this poem while listening to me play the hammered dulcimer, an instrument with more than sixty strings played with small hammers like those on the inside of the piano. I was playing a Celtic tune from Ireland called "Si Bheag, Si Mhor." The melody is a waltz, which means it includes three musical beats per line, just like much of Devon's poem.

But the music wasn't solely responsible for the rhythm; if it had been, every line would have come out in three feet. Devon was listening to the music, but she was also listening to the images the music evoked and the rhythm that felt right for her words.

Writing in Time

Before you try writing poems in rhythm with your class, try listening to different kinds of music and counting the beats. Classical music that changes tempo and rhythm often would work well for this exercise, as would jazz or African drumming. Don't worry about following every change of rhythm in the music, just listen to a whole piece and then ask your students what kinds of rhythm they heard, and whether the tempo (the speed of the music) changed or remained the same.

You can also play this simple rhythm game with a group. Have eight students stand in a circle. First, try clapping together while counting to eight several times. Then have each student clap once while saying a number out loud; go in order around the circle from one to eight. When you reach eight, you should start over with one, clapping twice this time around. Now you have sixteen notes in eight beats. You can go on to clapping three or more times for each number or beat.

If the students are finding this easy, think of other ways to subdivide the eight beats. Each student, for instance, can imagine two claps but only actually clap the second time. You might skip certain people or add others in and see what happens. What's it like to play this game with only three people in the circle, or with eleven? Does the rhythm seem to flow more or less naturally?

Popular music from our part of the world mostly uses measures with beats in multiples of four. Poetry written with four beats per line will thus sound very songlike; children's poems are often written this way. Suggest to your class that some poems might be more interesting with a regular rhythm made up of a different number of beats, or a rhythm in which the beats repeat in the same lines of each stanza.

For now, it's probably a good idea for your students not to try to rhyme, but instead just to concentrate on the beat of the lines. Remind them that they don't have to be slaves to the rhythm; reread Devon's poem to see how effective it can be to change the beats around in certain lines. Tell them to strive for an overall feeling, not just a bunch of singsongy lines. You might also want to invite them to play with the beats in their lines. Just because a line has only three beats doesn't mean it has to have three words or syllables— it can just as easily have five, six, or seven words.

If you want to offer a few ideas for subjects for these poems, try asking your students to consider the following questions before they write:

What rhythms does your body naturally offer you when you move, breathe, eat, or work? What parts of your body do you use to create rhythm?

Think about the difference in rhythm when you walk, skip, jump, and run. How do those rhythms reflect the type of activity with which you associate these actions?

What role does tempo play in your life? Can you think of a time when you intentionally wanted things to happen faster or more slowly?

The following poem is a sonnet written to fourteen words supplied by the class. (I mentioned this assignment in the unit of this chapter on sound.) The teacher who wrote this sonnet had been to a jazz performance within a few hours of her composing it. Notice the way she picked up on the rhythms of the music in her poem. If you read this poem aloud, it almost sounds like a chant.

Jazz Man

Jazz Man gonna make that juke joint jump
Over under around and through the rainbow.
Man, can that cat jam!
Jammin' and clammin' and slammin,' the clamor

Like a fish
Beboppin' and floppin' just to live.
Dig that dude, the beat is his.
Watch him take that low dive.

Thump!
Left hand takes the bass in stride, while the melody soars
like a butterfly
And the bass goes bump, bump, bum ka-bump.
Hey, baby. Beautiful!

I'm hypnotized, I'm mesmerized, I'm glued right to my chair.
Cool, man. Hot jazz! What you played, what I heard.

-Terry Starr, teacher

Follow-up Activities

1. Try writing with your class to a metronome. You can set the tempo at any speed you wish. Then let that tempo guide you while you write. Again, don't become a slave to the beats; use your own judgement about when to adhere closely to the rhythm and when to break away

from it. Try doing two or three fast-writes this way, and then discuss the results with the class.

2.   Combine rhythm and rhyme to write sonnets, villanelles, sestinas, or rhyme royal. Tell your students to be very careful that neither the rhythm nor the rhyme scheme forces them to create an awkward or unnecessary line. These forms are some of the hardest in the English language, and if your students just spill out lines that rhyme but don't make much sense, they're not taking full advantage of the possibilities such forms offer.

3.   Line division also offers rhythm to a poem. Have your students take any poem they've written and change the line breaks (this is easy if the poem is on a computer). How has the rhythm changed? They might also take paragraphs of fiction and try to line them as poems, or even take a poem, type it out as a paragraph, and then ask someone else to create line breaks for them.

INTERPRETATION

Writers reinterpret stories and ideas frequently. Thinking about how musicians use interpretation can free up your students to try this more often in their written works.

How many times do you suppose you've heard your favorite Christmas carols during your lifetime? Do you think you could count the number of times you've listened to "Jingle Bells" or "We Wish You a Merry Christmas"? Once a year, we trot out many of the same old songs to celebrate Christmas. (Even if you don't celebrate Christmas yourself, you probably know many of these songs by heart.) There's a good reason for this: they're catchy songs. Still, it's easy to get tired of the same melody played over and over, and that's all most of us really know of these songs—the melody.

More than likely, "Jingle Bells" was written on a particular instrument, such as the piano. Perhaps the composer of the song merely sang it the first time through. It doesn't much matter to me when I sing the song, because what's important about the song is the melody, the lyrics, and the performance of it—who I'm singing with and how. I have no qualms about playing any instrument I wish behind the singing, from guitar to kazoo. Why should I? This song has been performed in thousands (if not millions) of different ways over the years, on different instruments, at different speeds, and with different rhythms. Who's to say which way is best? Musicians have to ask themselves many questions each time they prepare to perform a piece of music. What combination of instruments will be used? How many times will the verses or choruses be repeated? Should there be any improvisation? What rhythm should the music follow?

"Jingle Bells," after these decisions have been made by a particular group of musicians, might be performed as a rap, with a reggae beat, on bagpipes and snare drum, or with the chorus repeated over and over and over. Interpretation is a large part of the artistic process. There's as much room for creativity in arranging a song as there is in writing one.

Experimenting with Arrangements
If you created some homemade instruments, this activity would be a good vehicle for using them. Otherwise, you can have students make music with objects they find around the room, with their voices, or with instruments they bring to class.

The exercise is simple. Have your students choose a song they all know well and have heard many times, and play it in a very different style than the way it's usually performed. Before you begin, you might want to brainstorm a list of songs to choose from. Here are a few examples:

Christmas carols: "Silent Night," "Rudolph," "White Christmas"

Children's songs: "Twinkle, Twinkle," "Row, Row, Row Your Boat," "Bingo"

Rock and pop songs: Whatever is popular and played often on the radio

Patriotic songs: "This Land Is Your Land," "America the Beautiful"

TV theme songs: Again, whatever everyone knows

Hymns: "Amazing Grace," "Jesus Loves Me"

Divide your students into ensembles and ask each group to choose one song. Then give them some time to work on their performance. As they prepare the music, they should consider the following questions:

How fast should we play this song?

What rhythm might make the song different or more interesting?

What instruments (if any) do we want to use?

Will we sing or just play instruments?

How will we begin and end the piece?

Should everyone play all of the time, or should different instruments and voices come in and out of the music?

Do we need a conductor?

When they're ready, have the ensembles perform for the rest of the class. Then discuss the choices each group of musicians made. What was effective? What didn't work? How would the groups do things differently the next time?

Interpretation in Writing

Writers reinterpret other works and ideas all the time. Most of Shakespeare's plays were interpretations of older stories, historical episodes, or legends. Poets return to the same subjects again and again—myths, Bible stories, even other poems.

It might be best for students to start by applying the process of interpretation to one of their own works. Have your students find a poem or story they've already written and reinterpret it. This is much the same as changing the voice of the work (as I suggested in the unit called "The Singing Voice"), but it might also include changing the format (making a poem a story or vice versa), writing from a new point of view, or telling the story within a different time frame.

Your class might also try writing an interpretation of a work by another poet or writer. Pick a great story or an episode captured by a piece of writing and write it again in your own way. Try to make it as different from the original as possible.

Here's a passage from a story that takes a very famous written work and writes it again with a new voice. The original story is the tale of Rumpelstiltskin, but this student set the familiar story in a new context. Here, Rumpelstiltskin speaks in street slang about his second visit to the king's castle:

Next day, I'm finally going to see the king, girl or no girl. I'm walking, I hear crying, I try to go on, but my heart melts. I got to stop. Same situation, only *this* time, if she succeeds, she gets to marry the king.

The room is *huge*, and I'm thinkin', "This is gonna take *all* day." I've already lost two days' business on this chick, so now she's gonna have to pay. So she promises me her first child, and I accept. I felt kinda' guilty, cause it's her kid and all, but hey, it gets lonely in the woods. I save her life again, she gets married, she has the kid, and I come to collect. Only Queenie doesn't want to give him up anymore!

-Coralie LeCoguic, 10th grade

Follow-up Activities

1. Try asking each member of your class to write about the same subject or event in a different style, form, or voice. Assign a student "conductor" to oversee the project and make sure that each person offers a different interpretation. When the pieces are done, read them all consecutively and discuss the results. Which approach worked best? Which worked least well? Why?

2. Titles make a good starting place for a new interpretation of another work of art. Have your students look through some poetry books and find a few titles. Then use those titles for new poems they write. Here are a few examples I took from an English literature anthology of poems written before 1800: "On a Girdle," "A Valediction: Forbidding Mourning," "The Phoenix and The Turtle," "The Castaway," "The Universal Prayer." Any of these might spark an interesting new work.

3. You can find some interesting examples of interpretation by listening to musicians like Ella Fitzgerald or Louis Armstrong singing Gershwin and Cole Porter songs; Aaron Copland's version of a Shaker song in *Appalachian Spring;* or Peter, Paul & Mary singing songs written by Bob Dylan. Listen to some of these or other interpretations of older music with your students and ask them whether or not it's important to know the original source. Does it change the way you listen to the music? Is this also true of literature? Have your students find the older sources of some familiar literature like Shakespeare's plays, Yeats' "Leda and the Swan," or T. S. Eliot's "The Wasteland."

IMPROVISATION

Improvisation may be an exciting technique for your writing students to explore, since the idea of using words quickly and freely is one they may not have encountered before. If you've ever watched jazz musicians make up the music they're playing as they go along, you may have asked the following question: *How do they know what to play?* Making up music isn't as simple as picking up an instrument and playing a bunch of random notes—try it and you'll see. Nor is it as easy as whistling a tuneless melody while you work or drive.

But there *is* one important rule to improvisation, even though over the years it's been stretched (as most artistic rules eventually are) by musicians seeking to create new types of music and ways of thinking about music. This rule is fundamentally the same whether you're improvising a jazz solo, a bluegrass riff, a rock-and-roll guitar melody, or a classical cadenza.

The important rule is this: *Follow the structure as it's been laid out.* Exactly *how* you follow it—what notes you think go with the structure that you're working with—is a matter for debate. Blues musicians improvise differently from traditional Irish musicians, even when the underlying structure is remarkably similar. In most forms of music, players improvise by beginning with a well-known melody or song. That way, anyone can play along, and the structure is familiar. From there, it's just a matter of deciding what notes to put in (sometimes called *ornamentation*) and what notes to leave out. You can also improvise by changing the length of notes, the volume, the pitch (several pitches will often work in the same spot), and the rhythm.

For some musicians, improvisation is intimidating, frightening, and revealing. It's also what makes a lot of musicians feel alive. Like drama and dance, music that involves improvisation exists entirely in the moment, and mistakes and moments of genius pass by quickly. That's what makes improvisation exhilarating and terrifying at the same time.

Recognizing Structure

Most musicians improvise by listening to and playing along with chords (any group of three or more notes played at once). You don't have to be able to identify or even understand chords to appreciate improvised music. It's easy enough to tell who's playing the chords—usually the guitar or piano player, but in general anyone playing multiple notes instead of a solo melody line. Bass players and rhythm players often back this up, even during other musicians' solos.

Listen to a jazz recording of someone like Louis Armstrong or a bluegrass recording of Bill Monroe. You'll hear them improvise over chords. First, they'll play the melody as it was written. Then they'll alter it a little bit more the next time through, and even more the time after that. Eventually they'll come back to the original melody, though it may never be played in exactly the same way as the first time.

You can easily experiment with improvisation using rhythm instruments. Just have one student start and keep a steady rhythm (not just one beat over and over, but an interesting series of beats). Then let other students try playing with and against that rhythm with other instruments, changing it a little each time.

You can also try improvising while you sing. Pick an easy song and ask one of your students to sing it aloud. Then have another student sing it, but this time ask the class how it should be changed. Should there be more notes or fewer? Should it be louder or softer? Try it several times, each time changing at least one part of the melody just a bit. If your students seem self-conscious about singing aloud, have them recite a rhyming poem or a rap song, and then make some changes to the way the words are spoken.

Improvisation

As in music, there's a difference between composition and improvisation in writing. Composition is what writers do all the time—they sit down with an idea or feeling and put down some words to express it.

For improvisation, you'll need a structure. This is especially fun with a group, since you can compare your results with those of other people. Here are a few suggestions for ways to improvise with your students. The results might be silly or serious or somewhere in between.

Improvisation on a Line of Poetry

This exercise can be used with poems by other writers or from students in your class. First, you'll need to find a few good, long lines (two or three lines together that make up one sentence will work well). I often use Dylan Thomas poems, since the language is so interesting in his work. Give the line to a student or pair of students, and give them a time interval in which to use only the words in the lines they've been given to create a poem. If you like, specify a number of lines (five to ten should be enough) to compose. Repeating words is okay, but no words can be added that are not in the original lines.

Round Robin Stories

Have your students complete this exercise in groups of four or five. Every student, on a separate sheet of paper, should write down a single sentence or line of poetry. Each student then passes the paper to his or her left, so that everyone now has a paper showing one sentence or line written by a neighbor. The second person adds a second line, then passes it to the left again. The papers go around the circle a couple of times, so that at the end, there are the same number of stories (or poems) as there are people in the group.

"Chord Chart" Syntax Poems

Since lots of chord progressions use only a few chords repeated in various ways, you can create a similar effect using parts of speech. Have your class create a "chord chart" made up of nouns, verbs, adjectives, and adverbs. If you want, throw in a couple of interjections or conjunctions. Each student should write a poem that uses the appropriate parts of speech in the appropriate places. You needn't specify every word's part of speech, and filler words can be used, but every part of speech you specify *should* be used. Here's a pattern for chord chart poems and two examples:

> Noun / noun / like / noun
> adjective / noun / verb / noun
> noun / adjective / noun
> noun / verb/ noun / adjective
> adjective / adjective / adjective
> noun / conjunction / noun / conj. / noun
> verb / conj. / verb / conj. / verb
> like / 1st noun / 2nd noun / preposition / noun
> preposition / noun / preposition / noun.

Rainbows

Rainbows, rainbows, like music
    swirling colors sweep sky
      spectrum apprenticed to atmosphere
        This is the way music functions
Fictional, actual, actionable,
    notes and grooves and shapes
   bend and arch and flow
  like rainbows, rainbows over sky,
      under sky, around sky.

-Mark Niels, 10th grade

Night Syntax

Trees and grass like carpet,
    flowing trees bend in the breeze.
   Night sounds softer than whispers.
      I have been thinking of you dreaming.
Blue, green, red,
    dreams of hands and fingers
   touch and smooth and soothe
  like trees and grass against air,
     against the ground, against the night.

-Corey Framer, 10th grade

Follow-up Activities

1. Listen to some jazz artists improvise: Charlie Parker, John Coltrane, Wynton Marsalis, Bobby McFerrin. You might also listen to improvisation by groups like The Grateful Dead or the recent rock band Phish, or blues musicians like B.B. King or Muddy Waters. Then ask your students to improvise with words based on a line from one of these songs, the title of a piece, or some feeling or idea they get while listening to the music itself. Their pieces should focus on starting with the music and then on changing the idea or

set of words in a few ways to produce different lines, sounds, or moods.

2. Fast-writing uses a process fairly similar to improvisation in music. While fast-writing involves composition, it also asks the writer to focus on a specific topic for a short length of time, to explore the variations and possibilities of that topic in words. Try asking your students to fast-write without offering a topic. Simply time them for five or ten minutes and tell them to write about absolutely anything, even if the result is just a list of objects in the room or sounds they hear. Then take these fast-writes and find a line or an idea in them to work with and improvise on until a polished poem or story emerges.

Chapter Three

On Stage

ACTING AND PERFORMANCE

*A*cting exercises involve social skills that help kids learn to get along and work together. They involve communication and interaction, the benefits of which should be clear to writing teachers. They encourage students to think about story development, characters, voices, and description. They also encourage practical skills such as planning, cooperation, and performing or speaking before a group.

Many of the techniques and elements of drama included in this chapter are presented as fun activities or games, and they should be orchestrated in that way. It's important, however, not to consider them as games in which there's a winner or loser. Competition doesn't belong in these exercises; they're about group work and ensemble performance. When it comes time to write, your students shouldn't be saddled with the idea that other members of the class are "better" or "worse" at acting than they are. You can have your students write plays, write about plays, and write in response to acting and creating theater. All are valuable, and none should be overlooked as a possible source of inspiration.

As you read this chapter, think about the possibilities drama and acting offer to writers. It's not just about learning technical skills, though that's important. Acting offers a chance to bring words to life, as well. That's a chance no writer should be willing to pass up.

CHARACTER

Like writers, actors try to create fiction by changing themselves. Writers do this with words, by creating speakers, narrators, and characters. Actors do it by creating characters too, and though they may have slightly different concerns than writers (an actor's audience actually hears and sees the character, while readers supply a good deal from the imagination), the process is very much the same.

Every character, whether invented by a writer or an actor, comes from that real person's experience and observations. You can change your appearance, your accent, your clothing, or your demeanor, but there's always something about you that remains the same. You can't change everything, and who would want to? A blank slate, like a robot, would have no personal experience to bring to a character.

Because personal experience is such an important part of creating believable characters, a lot of actors try to replicate the experiences of the characters they play. This is sometimes called "method acting." If an actor is going to play a grocery store clerk, he or she might actually work at a grocery store for a few days. Writers don't always have this luxury. Sometimes a single story or poem will contain many characters, and all of them have to be believable.

So how does a writer develop believable characters?

Well, there are other ways for an actor *or* a writer to explore different kinds of voices, people, and traits. Observation is a good place to start. Imagination helps. A sense of humor or a talent for imitation are also helpful.

But most important, your own experience and memories provide a great resource for understanding the experiences of others. Acting begins with changing yourself, but changing yourself begins with understanding who you are and how you got to be that way.

Character Development

Have your students observe people for a week. Every day, as they enter your class, ask them to write a brief, anonymous character description or trait on a Post-it-size note and stick it to a certain wall or bulletin board. Have each student include a description of himself or herself on one of the days, but make sure the students don't tell their classmates (or you) which of the descriptions applies to them.

At the end of the week, read through the notes as a class. Then put them all in a hat and have various students pick one at random. You might have students pick one at a time or in small groups, but in either case, the students should immediately act out a brief scenario involving the character and let the rest of the class guess what is happening. You can also guess which character descriptions directly refer to people in the class.

Then do a short, timed fast-write in which students create a brief character based on one of the descriptions. Read a couple of these aloud, and then ask your class the following questions:

What does it take to develop a well-rounded character? Where does the individuality of that character begin? In actions? In speech? In emotions?

Is it easier to develop a character to act out based on one movement, one line of dialogue, or a general description of that character's job or activities?

What is the difference, if there is one, between writing a character and acting one out? What do you need to know in each case as the artist and as the audience? What are the benefits and drawbacks of using performance and words to create characters?

After you share your initial fast-writes, talk about what you liked and what didn't seem to work. Then create a list of interesting details or items that might be included in a character description. Brainstorm freely and make a list on the board of all the things you might want to know about a character. Here's a list of ideas for information about a female character compiled by a class I taught recently:

Job—what does she do?
Where does she live? In a house? A cave? On a boat?
What does her hair look like? Her nose? Her fingernails?
What does she most want?
What does she least want?
What does she fear?
How does she get to work?
What was her grandmother's name?
Does she collect anything?
What's her favorite animal? Favorite color? Favorite dessert?

As you can see, the list could go on and on. The specific elements aren't nearly as important as the quality of the ideas; details and traits that develop the character's originality are what make for fresh description.

Try having your students compile lists about two people—one real (a relative or friend) and one fictitious (a historical character might also work well). Then have them write poems or short prose pieces in which they explore those characters. A good idea for revision is to have a student write the same piece again in a different voice, switching from first person, say, to second or third person.

You might also encourage your students to write about themselves as characters (like actors making their own characters an extension of themselves; not everything has to be true, but that's where the description should start). Have them write self-descriptions in second or third person.

The following excerpt is from a story written by a girl, though the narrator is a boy. The author created a female character by trying to see herself from another point of view.

> Ruth was a shy girl with long hair who lived next door to us, with green eyes, a taste for flowing clothes, white skin, and the aim of an Olympic archer with insults. She stored up barbs, condemnations, and invectives like a hoard of dolls, took them out and played with them now and then. In school she listed insults in the back of her notebook, saving them for later use. She was deadly with her timing and accuracy. On the bus one afternoon she called my brother "common baggage," and after we all stared at her for a moment, she merely shrugged and named her source: "Shakespeare."
>
> For all that, Ruth Winson was lovely, and I lay awake nights thinking of her. There were even times I believed the insults she turned on me were a form of flattery. The shape of her, the sound of her voice— these things rattled in my head when dreams wouldn't. I knew how to store things up myself.
>
> *-Ruth Winson, 10th grade*

Follow-up Activities

1. Pick one student to be a director, and have everyone else stand out of sight but within earshot. The students should line up and walk out into view of the director one at a time. Before each student appears, the director will call out a character—"policeman," "teacher," "revolutionary," or "idiot," for example—and the student who appears must enter the stage area in the role of that character. Give the direc-

tor a few minutes to brainstorm characters before beginning. After everyone's had a turn, have each student do a fast-write in the voice of the character he or she was assigned. Have the director write in his or her own voice.

2. Make a character deck by drawing or writing short descriptions on blank playing cards cut from poster board (involve your students in this process). Then have your students play "character poker," in which small groups are dealt hands of cards and then can bargain and trade with each other. Once the students have the hands they want (or are stuck with), they must write scenes that include all of their characters (five is a good number).

3. Find some random character descriptions from best-selling and classic novels and read just a paragraph from each to your class. Discuss which are best and which are worst, and why. Then ask them to pick the worst of the descriptions (include a few from romance novels) and rewrite them so they're much more interesting and original.

THE SPEAKING VOICE

Each of your students uses a particular voice in his or her writing; from drama exercises, your students can learn more about how to use that voice and also how voices add to character development. Actors develop what's called a *stage voice*. This is a voice that sounds natural even though it's intended to project enough for audiences to hear everything that's said. It allows an actor to whisper or shout, or at least to convey the impression of whispering or shouting, without leaving the audience wondering what in the world the actor said.

Practice stage voices with your class. First, loosen your tongues by saying a few tongue twisters as a group. Choose some of your favorites ("Peter Piper" and "Sally sells seashells," for instance), and then ask if anyone in the class knows an unusual tongue twister or would like to make one up. Also, exercise your vocal muscles by reciting the vowels, numbers, or alphabet together loudly, then softly (but clearly), then in a normal voice.

When you're ready, find an area of the room to serve as a stage and set up the scene as if it were a restaurant. (You could also imitate a school cafeteria, a bus stop, or a movie ticket line.) Have the class choose a line for one of two characters sitting at a table to say about a third character sitting at another table. The line should be whispered in a stage voice, and should be insulting or personal, such as "Can you believe that woman's hair?" or "Boy, that guy can pack away a lot of food." Have one of the characters speak the line a couple of different times and see if it sounds at all natural. If anyone in the room doesn't hear the line, he or she should shout "do it again!" and the actor must repeat the line so it's audible.

Then have everyone write a line for the scene on a folded piece of paper. The lines can be funny or crazy, but they ought to make sense within the context of the scene. (If you like, give the other actor a line of dialogue to set this line up.) Drop the lines in a pile on the table and have an actor or several actors try them out one at a time. Again, if anyone can't hear the line, he or she is welcome to shout out "do it again!" and make the actor try once more.

After playing this game, ask your students whether the lines were at all believable. If any line was not believable, was it because of the line itself or the way it was delivered? How might it be delivered differently?

Try asking other students to speak the same lines and make them sound completely different. Tell them they can change the volume, tone, enunciation, direction, or emotion in their voices. Then try the same lines in different accents or dialects.

When your class is ready, have them consider the following questions before writing:

Has there ever been a time when the volume or tone of what someone said to you conveyed more meaning than what was actually said? What was the context? Remember the details of that encounter.

Have you ever overheard anything you weren't intended to? How did it make you feel? How did you physically react?

Imagine a scene in which a character might use a false or an assumed voice for some reason. Imagine a scene in which what's meant is not the same as what's said. What are the details of this scene?

Remember or imagine a time when you spoke to someone with a different accent or dialect. What possible miscommunications or humorous misunderstandings might arise in such a scene?

Have your students write poems or stories that include lines spoken by characters or descriptions of the way characters speak. Tell them to pay particular attention to how the lines are spoken. You might note that this isn't necessarily an exercise in dialogue; a whole poem might contain just one telling spoken line.

I remember a time when I was twelve years old and my brother, home from college, had brought a friend of his who came from Paris.

His name was Alain and I fell in love with his "artiste" air and his magnificent, deep black eyes. I decided I would impress him by speaking French only throughout the dinner he would attend.

I practiced in front of the mirror for several days before the big evening, and when it came I was stoked and a little nervous. I was pounding out "The Mexican Hat Dance" on the piano when he and my brother graced us with their presence. I jumped up.

"Bonjour!" I greeted them confidently. "Voulez-vous une boisson?" ("Hello, would you like a drink?") Alain looked at me with a slightly bemused expression. I blushed furiously—he was impressed already!

I followed him around the rest of the evening, chattering in my impeccable French. I was on cloud nine.

I saw Alain and my brother out, and as I turned to go I heard Alain say, "What a lovely little sister you have. And her Spanish accent—oh, très bien!"

-Rachel Dart, 8th grade

Follow-up Activities

1. Ask your class to write poems that are also tongue twisters, with ridiculously heavy alliteration. Try to keep them from becoming *too* ridiculous, but also let them be light-hearted or funny. When they're finished, read them aloud.

2. Have your students pretend they're at a party and ask them to circulate through the room talking to one another. As they're doing so, they should follow one rule: every conversation must be about someone else in the room. Caution them to keep the game from becoming personal or downright mean; you might set some limits before you start. After you've played this game for a while, stop and talk about how it made different people feel or think. Then do a fast-write based on those feelings and what was said to evoke them.

3. Look for interesting dialect and accents in the words spoken by characters in plays your students have read. You might also read lines from plays by Langston Hughes, August Wilson, Brian Friel, or Tennessee Williams, and discuss how accent and dialect affect the words and the actor's ability to deliver them convincingly.

USING THE BODY

In this unit, your students will think about the body and how important it can be for a writer trying to create or describe a character or an emotion. There are parts of my body I almost never think about, unless I hurt myself or have to perform some highly unusual action. My elbows, for instance. My heels. The backs of my knees. Other parts I use and think about every day. My eyes are weak, so I wear glasses that are a constant nuisance if it rains or if I want to play a sport. I use my fingers to make a living—to type and to play instruments—so I take care of my hands. My back can easily start to ache, so I have to be careful when I lift things.

Think of the simple actions you perform every day: raising a coffee mug, answering a telephone, writing a letter. The physical manipulation of your body required to perform these tasks is actually quite complicated and precise. Your brain must coordinate the actions of many body parts at once to control the way you walk, eat, breathe, play a sport, cook a meal, or drive a car.

Most of us take simple movement for granted. Actors don't, and neither do dancers. Our bodies communicate a great deal about how we feel, what we think, and how we will act; stage performers, whose job is to communicate such ideas and feelings, must be aware of what messages they send with their bodies. Does this mean controlling every part of the body at all times? Probably not. What it *does* mean is becoming aware of how different body parts move and react, and how that *looks*.

Read the following poem, and notice how its speaker tries to capture both the sense of abandonment of control in the dance and the way in which the whole body and all its parts contribute to expression:

Thursday Night

Palms fingertips twitch
sway shimmy shine biting lips and sweetly

pained shut eyes
fragrance of bodies limbs in perpetual motion hips slipping
into the weather worn denim of
music
squealing silver diva in cupped hands
sings
a black panther poised to pounce
drums cymbals a rattlesnake in the tall grass
sweat glowing
foreheads cheeks elbows arms hands in air twisting back
and forth a multitude a slap clapping chorus
electric free spirits
twelve bar
deep blue righteousness.

-Elizabeth Kirkindall, 11th grade

The dancers in Elizabeth's poem use more than just their legs or arms; they use "foreheads" and "cheeks" and "elbows," parts of the body we might not immediately associate with dance. These dancers aren't, of course, trying to control every small movement. In fact, the poem implies a release of absolute control. But the dancers are using parts of the body together, creating an expression through the movement of small elements such as palms and fingertips.

Pay close attention, while you read the remainder of this unit, to the parts of your body. Notice how they work together, how they react to one another, and under what conditions you use them individually. You might be surprised at the complexity of movements you barely even notice.

Focusing on the Body

For this exercise, play some soft music in the background. Whatever you choose, it shouldn't be too fast or loud.

To begin with, along with your students, just stretch and loosen a few of your body parts. Reach your arms out, up above your head, and down to your sides. Roll your shoulders forward and backward, and then roll your head. Stand on your toes. Bend your knees. Flex your fingers, wrists, and arms. Stretch any other part of your body you can think of.

When your students are relaxed and comfortable, give them a couple of simple tasks. First, have them choose one body part with which they perform some simple activity every day. Ask them to close their eyes and mime this activity. Do this a couple of times.

Now have the students open their eyes and find a partner. Each partner should now share the activity he or she chose by miming it for the other person. The viewer ought to guess what the first person is doing.

After everyone has shared, have the partners combine the two activities into one movement or set of movements, but this time ask them to make the gesture artistic, to give it some kind of meaning or message. Give the pairs a few minutes to work on this—you may meet with initial questions and confusion from students who don't "get it." Just repeat the instructions; eventually, most people figure out that you're not going to tell them what *meaning* is, that they have to decide that for themselves.

When the pairs have rehearsed their movements (which can involve both partners or just one), ask for volunteers to share with the class. Don't allow any explanation before the performance. Instead, have the partners show the class their activity or series of gestures, and then ask the class to comment. What's going on? What's attractive about the movements? How do the movements make you feel or think, and why?

This simple activity opens two doors for possible discussion. First of all, it forces the students to think about one body part and how we use it. By extension, it shows how varied and important the functions of each part of our body are.

Second, this exercise gets students thinking about the equation of movement with meaning. How do our body parts work alone or together to convey messages about emotions and ideas? That question, of course, is at the heart of dance.

After you've finished talking about how simple movements can become meaningful, prepare your students to write by asking them to choose a hand, a foot, a finger, an arm, or a leg and move it in all of the ways they can think of. Tell them to move that body part both generally and in specific ways, as if they were performing a particular task.

Then have each student make a list of functions, movements, and physical images that relate to that one body part. As they make the lists, suggest a few items to include by asking the following questions:

What will it feel like to move that body part when you're much older? How did it feel when you were much younger?

How will the appearance of that part of your body change over time?

What profession might use that part of the body most?

Did you inherit any peculiarities or quirks that have to do with this part of your body?

When the lists are done, suggest that each student write a poem or story that features that one part of the body. These works may include a description of someone else, of the student, or just generally of the part of the body. The works ought to focus on describing how that part moves and how it functions, and also use that movement to get across some message.

> Some people's hands are pretty—they have long thin fingers that end in perfect nails. These are the kinds of hands that wear slender bands of silver with tiny jewels in soft tones. My hands are not like these.
>
> Mother's hands are oldish, gentle and soft when they caress your cheek, and father's hands are calloused from typing out things. My sister's hands are smooth and soft, she will grow into them and then I will buy her a band of silver with a pastel jewel.
>
> My hands are not pretty, the fingers are more like short twigs, and the nails are frayed. Always the tips of my fingers are picked at and they bleed occasionally.
>
> Someday I will wrap my hands in bandages and cure them of their cuts. I will wait until they are soft and the skin is bright pink. Then I will have hands to be proud of, and I can wear a silver band with a jewel, but not a pastel one. Someday I will wear rings so that my fingers will sparkle as they dance out songs on the piano.
>
> But someday is a never word.
>
> *-Jennifer Rosenbaum, 8th grade*

Getting in touch with the functions, abilities, and movements of the body is one of the first tasks for any actor or dancer. It ought to be just as important to writers. Our bodies help us to communicate, to act, and to feel, and that's what writing is all about.

Follow-up Activities

1. Have your students move behind a mask so that the rest of the class can't see the performer's face. Each performer should try to convey an emotion or state without using the face. How hard is it? Which

emotions are easiest to convey? What other parts of your body do you most rely on to get the message across? After you play this game, have the students write a piece about communicating without using the face.

2.   Have students write poems about themselves as seen through someone else's eyes. What parts of their bodies stand out? Which parts are ignored or overlooked? How do other people, and especially those of the opposite sex, view their bodies? This exercise might be difficult for students who are self-conscious about their weight or appearance; if you wish you can tell your class to concentrate on positive aspects of their physical appearance.

M O N O L O G U E

Here's a passage from a monologue called "I am Hannah Szenes." The piece was written by a high school student in Tennessee, but the speaker is a young Hungarian involved in World War II:

> We are not soldiers, rather we are five young Jewish farmers from the kibbutzim. It is a beautiful night and we fly over Nazi-occupied Yugoslavia. The air is cool and listens to my thoughts as I prepare for our jump. It was about two months ago when we asked the British army to let us go on our mission. We will parachute into Yugoslavia and organize the resistance fighters who are scattered throughout the country. Small knives are embedded in our shirts, our handkerchiefs have drawn maps, our shirt buttons are tiny compasses, and we carry guns, radio equipment, important documents, and bombs. I am ready to jump.
>
> *-Rachel Bloomekatz, 10th grade*

Imagine acting out this passage. What movements would you include? How would you alter your voice, expressions, and clothing? To whom might you be speaking?

Actors frequently use monologues to audition for parts, but that's not the only reason to perform a piece with just one person on stage. There's a certain amount of liberty in speaking directly to the audience. For one thing, the character can explain his or her thoughts and actions without the explanation seeming contrived or unnatural. For another, a piece with just one actor often relies on words as much as on movement and action, and therefore the speaking part is given more attention by the audience (this ought to appeal to writers, who want their words to be heard and appreciated). Also, a monologue is an easy piece to produce; the actor only has to rehearse with himself or herself, and elaborate sets are usually deemed unnecessary.

Monologues, of course, have been a staple of poets for hundreds of years. Many of the same reasons apply: the character has a chance to speak directly to the audience, the voice of the character becomes extremely important, and the focus of the piece is narrowed so that details may be explored more fully. But a great written monologue won't necessarily be great when it's performed on stage by an actor, and a great stage monologue doesn't always translate well onto the printed page.

That doesn't mean actors and writers can't learn from one another how to create an interesting character with a compelling voice. Writers can make the language of a monologue more interesting, and actors can translate that language into real action, movement, and speech. By learning how an actor approaches such a task, the writer can then create more compelling and believable voices.

Bringing Monologues to Life

Start this unit by reading a few classic poems that might serve as monologues with your class. I suggest Tennyson's "Ulysses," Browning's "My Last Duchess," Marvell's "To His Coy Mistress," and a couple of recent works like Margaret Atwood's "You Begin" or Ishmael Reed's "I Am A Cowboy in The Boat of Ra."

As you read each of these pieces, ask yourself or your students a few questions. What do we know about the speaker from what he or she says? Can we determine appearance, voice, attitude, emotions? To whom is the speaker addressing these lines? What might the likely reply be?

Put your students in pairs and assign one poem to each pair. Give them a few minutes to work up a performance in which one student reads the text of the poem while the other acts out what is happening physically. The students can switch roles partway through the poem if they wish. Have them perform these pieces for the rest of the class, and then discuss the transition from written poetry to oral and physical interpretation. Does it change the meaning? Does it make things clearer or more ambiguous?

Now pose the following question to your students: What makes a good monologue? There are many answers—so many that you might want to put your students into groups and let them brainstorm lists with each other before you make a list of answers as a class. The answers are likely to include a lot of items such as interesting language, a strong character, a good dramatic situation, and an unseen but obvious audience.

All of these elements of monologue, however, really serve one purpose. They all allow the writer or the actor to gradually reveal something about the character or situation that has been hidden. This might be an idea, a background, a feeling, or an action. Look back at the poems I mentioned above and you'll see that as each develops, the reader can gradually piece together more bits and pieces about the speaker.

Monologues work much like scenes in courtroom drama in which a witness breaks down on the stand; in general, the more a person talks, the more he or she reveals about himself, either wittingly or unwittingly. Not many people are clever enough to talk on and on about themselves or things they've done and not reveal elements of their own character.

When your students start to write monologues, they should ask themselves these questions:

What is the situation and context of this scene? What does the speaker look, sound, act, and think like?

Who is the audience? Is it a single person or a group? What does the audience think of the speaker at the start? At the end?

What do I know about this character that the audience doesn't? How will I reveal that information to the audience?

If your students have an idea for a monologue already, they should begin writing immediately. They might find characters in a book, an artwork, or a school activity that they want to use as speakers. They might use the character decks I mentioned in the unit on character development. Otherwise, here's an exercise to help them start developing speakers.

First, hand out one blank index card to each student. On this card, the students should list their age, gender, race, hair color, any distinguishing features, religious beliefs, family relationships, and a few other personal items. Then, next to each of these items, have them write down a trait or characteristic that is very different from the one they used to describe themselves.

Give them a minute to consider these new items of description. Can they think of a person in a particular time or place whom some of these characteristics might describe? How would that person think and feel? Which of the items might be applicable and which might they need to change?

Have your students imagine or choose characters and write monologues in either poetic or prose forms that reveal something that is hidden about that character. Remind them to try to simulate the character's real voice as closely as possible, but not to be afraid to take some liberties with what the character might have actually said.

Follow-up Activities

1. Have your students find monologues they wrote earlier and try rewriting them in second or third person. Do they lose their effectiveness, gain, or remain pretty much the same? Now tell them to try writing a poem they originally wrote in second or third person as a monologue in first person.

2. Ask your class members to read a monologue like those I mentioned above and write another monologue, this time from the point of view of someone in the audience. They might choose to write as Ulysses' wife or son, the duchess in Browning's poem, or the woman to whom Marvell's speaker addresses his words.

3. There are very good monologues for high school students in plays like Wilder's *Our Town* and Miller's *The Crucible.* Have your students perform monologues from plays like these, and then have them try rewriting the scenes as poems or writing their own monologues for performance.

DIALOGUE

Writing teachers often send students out to record real dialogue—to eavesdrop on conversations between actual people. What these students rarely do, however, is write down more than the *words* of the dialogue.

Actors must consider how a character might change tone, volume, expression, and emphasis to convey the meaning of a line; these are important factors whether the line is delivered to one person or a thousand. But in a dialogue between two people (or in a small group conversation), the actor must also consider other factors: his or her position relative to the other people involved, body language, eye contact. And what if the other person in the conversation speaks a foreign language, is a genius or a complete idiot, or just comes from a different part of town?

Here's an example. Read the following lines of dialogue to yourself:

"I think we're lost."
"I'm certain we're not."
"No, I think we're lost."

This could be a pleasant conversation taking place between two friends. Or it could be a bitter and angry quarrel between two strangers trying to find their way off of a tropical island populated with angry natives. It could be a philosophical conversation about the nature of mankind.

How can tell you the difference? One method used by writers is to include *speaker tags,* which not only tell you who is speaking but also how:

"I think we're lost," Jack said.
"I'm certain we're not," answered Jill.
"No," said Jack, "I think we're lost."

Speaker tags are useful, but are often used quite clumsily by beginning writers. It's easy to forget that most readers' eyes skim right over these tags, so it's okay to leave them out or use the word *said* often. A novice writer often overcompensates with this sort of prose:

"I think we're lost," Jack exclaimed nervously.
"I'm certain we're not," cried Jill with exuberance.
"No," Jack declared, "I think we're lost."

The result is pretty boring. There are other ways of giving some idea of what the words mean. Naturally, a long work will add context to this scenario:

Jack glanced behind them. The natives were trudging up the side of the volcano, still keeping pace. He looked back at Jill, who lugged the pail of water behind him.

"I think we're lost."

But what if you're an actor trying to deliver the same lines? The audience, of course, knows who is speaking, but you can't shout out "I said nervously" after every line. Nor can you rely on context; you may be acting on a blank stage, creating the scenery in the imagination of the audience.

One way to vary the effect of the line is to emphasize certain words. One actor might deliver the line as, "I *think* we're lost," while another might try, "I think we're *lost*," and yet another might say, *"I* think we're lost."

Another tack might be to change tone or volume. This would result in the difference between a whisper *("I think we're lost")* and a scream ("I THINK WE'RE LOST!!!").

Yet another way of changing the line's meaning might be to stand very close to another person. Here's the line with two different sets of stage directions for the actor to follow:

JACK: *(looks around wildly)* I think we're lost.

or

JACK: *(turns his back on Jill and pouts)* I think we're lost.

Getting familiar with ways of delivering lines of dialogue is good for a writer; it helps students, especially, rid themselves of adverbs that *tell* how a speaker feels and include description and dialogue that *shows* the same thing.

Try this experiment with your class. Have each student record one dialogue between two people not in the class. In addition to writing down the spoken words, the students should note how the speakers vary and use tone, volume, emphasis, body position and language, and eye contact. When you share the results, first have someone else in the class read only the dialogue the student recorded. Then let the student who did the recording read the same passage using the other observations he or she made. As a class, discuss the importance of these observations and how they change the meaning of what is said.

Practicing Dialogue

Choose a scene that involves two characters. The background for this scene might be a place in your school, a conversation between family members, or any other public place. Choose two students to start the scene, and allow them to improvise lines of dialogue for about two minutes. The result is not likely to be very interesting, but it will provide a starting point for the following exercises.

Now ask one of the students (or another in the class) to approach the same scene with a different motive than just talking. The motive might be to ask for something, to belittle the other person, to kiss up, or to make the person fall in love. Allow them to run through the scene a couple more times with different motives, and then ask the class to discuss the changes. Was the meaning changed merely by what was said, or also by physical movement, tone, volume, or other factors?

Now try structuring dialogue improvisations by asking pairs of students to create scenes that involve different ways of communicating with each other:

- Ask one pair of students to demonstrate a scene in which one person stands uncomfortably near another. Then change this scene so that the distance between two people is a problem for one of them.
- Another pair should create a scene in which a person talks uncomfortably loudly or softly.
- Another pair should use expressions that suggest opposite feelings of those presented in the actual words spoken.
- Another pair should use eye contact to add meaning to a scene.

After you've run through some of these physical ways of changing dialogue, try acting out scenes in which the tone, form, or manner of address changes the impact of the words. Set up scenes in which one actor uses sarcasm, moral authority, interruptions, silence, questions, or ridicule to load his or her replies with emotional context.

Once you've experimented with lots of ways of delivering dialogue, go back and look at some stories and poems that include dialogue. Is the dialogue always completely realistic? Should it be? What are some ways in which writers use the physical and vocal cues of characters to make dialogue more interesting and vivid?

Here's an example in which a sixth-grade student created three characters, each with a different agenda. In the story, which is set in ancient

Greece, these characters each speak with different tones of voice and with different emotions as they each try to accomplish certain goals.

> "I'm very, very sorry, but this child is just too weak," the government official said in a voice containing no remorse.
>
> This was a regular process for him. He was one of those who chose which babies were strong enough to live and which ones would be abandoned in the mountains. To him they were just soldiers and home-makers, all property of the government.
>
> "Please, please! You have taken two children of mine already up to the mountain you call a final resting place for these babies. I must be weak myself to bear these children so lacking in strength. Punish me and not them!"
>
> Helen advanced but was held back by her husband Marsyas. Helen asked to speak to another government official who happened to be her uncle. He was the one who made the final decision on who would go to the mountains.
>
> "Uncle Narcissus, I beg you to show mercy on my child!" Helen exclaimed.
>
> "You know I can't do that. It's against all rules in Sparta. Don't make this harder than it should be."
>
> "My mother took you into her home when you came back from battle without your shield and were looked upon as a coward."
>
> "If I claimed that the baby was strong, I would lose my job but there is something I can do for you."
>
> Uncle Narcissus told Helen of the place where they would abandon the babies.
>
> *- Elizabeth Johnson, 6th grade*

Ask your students to write a poem or story in which dialogue is used to propel the story, to illuminate the relationships between the characters, and to provide a context for physical communication as well. These pieces need not have lots of dialogue in them, but they should have enough to demonstrate a relationship that doesn't have to be explained to the reader.

Follow-up Activities

1. Have students write dialogue poems over days or weeks with a secret pen pal in the class. These works should respond to one another directly, and should be left in a place where either party can retrieve them without the other noticing, such as a central filing cabinet. At

the end of a given period, have the students get together with their partners and turn the pieces into one finished work.

2. Play dialogue checkers by having each student write down twelve lines of dialogue that are original or taken from a story or book you're reading. The lines should be written on different-colored slips and placed on a checkerboard. Students play checkers as normal, but at the end of the game, the winner chooses half of the lines he or she has left or has won and gives them to the loser. Each student then writes a piece that includes all of the lines he or she now has.

3. You can find interesting dialogue in just about any play that's well known. With your class, look at the way people speak in plays such as Chekhov's *Uncle Vanya*, Ibsen's *A Doll's House,* or Simon's *The Odd Couple.* Notice particularly how characters react to one another's lines and what is communicated without speaking aloud, and then discuss ways of using these techniques in your writing.

4. Look for some poems that include dialogue such as those by Frost, Yeats, or Browning. Does the dialogue feel natural or odd in metered, rhymed poetry? Try having your class write poems with some kind of form that also includes actual dialogue.

GIVE-AND-TAKE

Teamwork is a large part of what makes the arts so exciting. Besides the interaction between an artist and his or her audience, many art forms rely on ensemble performance. Music, dance, and drama often involve artists working together. In many performances, there are artists of all types involved, as well: dancers and actors on stage, visual artists making sets and costumes, writers preparing scripts, and musicians providing sound. Writers are sometimes robbed of this element of the artistic process, but in this unit your students may discover that writing can use teamwork as well as any art.

One reason most plays have a director is the same reason that classrooms have teachers and countries have presidents or kings; with one person in charge, the decision-making process is faster and, sometimes, more reliable. But there's no law that says a play must have a director. In fact, some of the most creative and interesting moments come from actors responding to one another in the moment of performance. Give-and-take between performers requires concentration, trust, and a willingness to adapt, but it's one of the most rewarding of performance experiences when an ensemble act of creativity occurs.

Working Together

Improvisation is a big part of working with a group. Even though you may be acting in a play in which each line is written beforehand and stage directions are explicit, the unexpected does happen. Sets break down, people forget their lines, audiences don't laugh where they're supposed to, and music doesn't always enter on cue.

The following exercises all use some degree of improvisation, although they're not always about being clever or creative quickly in emergencies. Rather, these exercises are about working with someone to put together a scene; they're about sending messages and communicating through language, eye contact, movement, and preparation. They shouldn't be seen as competitive exercises at all, but as games in which everyone has the same goal—to produce a cohesive scene. Try a few of these with your students and discuss the results:

Party Quirks: This game has become popular recently because it's been seen on television shows that feature improvisation. It involves at least two actors and can include many more. Everyone should write down one quirk someone at a party might have, including quite ridiculous traits or activities. A few suggestions might include having a cold, being a rock star, having fur all over your body, or acting like one of the Seven Dwarfs. One person pretends to be the host of the party, and one by one the actors pretend to arrive at the party displaying one of the quirks. The host guesses the quirk while staying in character by offering the actor something he or she needs or by otherwise demonstrating that the quirk has been revealed. When an actor's quirk is guessed, he or she leaves the stage.

Round Robin Scenes: In a round robin scene, only two actors at a time are on stage. They begin a normal scene, and continue acting until someone shouts "Freeze!" At that moment, both actors freeze, even if one is in the middle of a sentence or strange movement. The person who yelled runs on stage, taps one actor on the shoulder, and takes his or her place in exactly the same physical position. He or she then continues the scene in the first actor's place. At first, have your students maintain one story line as they try this exercise. Later you might allow them to change the story completely; this allows for very funny interpretations of positions and movements.

Props: Gather a collection of strange and interesting objects; you might have students bring some to class. Put your students in pairs and give each pair one object. Then tell them to come up with as many different scenes involving that object as possible. No scene should be longer than about fifteen seconds. Give the class five minutes to prepare, and then go around the room and have each pair of students do one scene at a time. The scenes can be funny or serious, but each should use the object in a completely different context.

Speaking Together: This game isn't actually about speaking *together* at all; it's about waiting for your chance to say your lines. Every student should have one line of dialogue ready. You can make these up or take them from other sources. One person stands and says his or her line. Anyone who thinks his or her line should come next (the lines should fit some context) stands up and says another line. The object is to let everyone say his or her line at least once. If any two people speak at one time, or if longer than five seconds passes between lines, the entire group has to start over. This game is a little easier if you insist that all lines deal with a similar subject, such as cars, a vacation, or a baseball game.

You can play one or all of these games, or you can make up your own. Some of your students may know others that involve working together, as well. The important point to remember is that none of these games should be a competition—they ought to inspire collaboration and ensemble activity.

Writing with an ensemble can also be rewarding. Have your students write both in ensembles and about them. Here are some ideas for writing assignments that involve thinking about ensembles:

Take one line from a poem or story you've written, or write a single line. Work with a group to put all of the lines into one cohesive piece.

Play a game of "freeze poetry." One person starts to write a poem on the chalkboard and continues until someone yells "Freeze!" That person then takes over and continues writing until someone else yells.

Write a piece about a group of people working together to accomplish something.

Find a strange or an interesting object and, with a partner, create a scene that involves that object. Write a piece that includes the object while your partner does the same. Share the results. You can also do this without inventing a shared scene first and see how closely your results match.

These are just examples of ensemble activities; you can probably come up with more. Allow your students to have fun with the creation of these works, but then have them return to the works and polish the drafts into more formalized poems and stories with some structure and cohesion.

Your writing class ought to be a place where people work as a group and enjoy the students with whom they're writing. Good writing won't happen without this feeling.

Here's an example of a piece in which each line was supplied by a different student. After a little bit of tinkering, the class arranged the lines to produce a poem.

Childhood
(A group poem)

I remember the smell of fresh dough and biscuits.
Outside, a rope swing fastened to tree branches
swayed in light wind.
Most times I was happy.
One night a storm blew in from across the pond.
The house gables shook and the shutters banged.
Nothing is safe when you're nine.
Most times I was not afraid.
The morning the geese had left their home,
flown away.
I remember my sister calling to me from the attic.
I went upstairs to look out the window.

A rainbow stretched across the sky.
I remember falling into adulthood like a stone.

-Class collaboration, 10th grade

Follow-up Activities

1. Have your students work together to produce a scene from an actual play. Give them enough time to prepare the scene and to memorize their lines. Hold a performance and let different groups perform the scenes for each other. Then talk about the challenges and benefits of working with others. Ask every student to write a creative reaction to the content of the scene or to the experience of working with others.

2. Put your students in groups and have them read each other's poems and make comments, suggestions, and changes to the works. This is an ongoing activity in every writing workshop I teach for any length of time. It demands that the group members are supportive, considerate, and serious about helping one another. Every piece should be treated with respect. Students don't have to accept each other's suggestions, but they do have to listen without being defensive.

MOVEMENT AND DANCE

Even performers who don't dance for a living need to be aware of how the body moves and the messages it conveys. Artistic movement, like other arts, is common to all cultures and people. That's because it's a fundamental way of releasing creative energy, expressing ideas, and having fun. When your students write, thinking about how their characters move can help make their poems and stories more interesting and more believable.

Ways of Moving

Look back at the earlier sections of this book called "Using the Body" and "Meter and Time." If parts of the body are *what* we use to move, and rhythm *when* we move, then space and energy are simply *where* and *how* we move.

Space, the *where* of dance, involves both the shapes the body forms and also the area it occupies. Find a place where your students can stand without touching one another or any objects (perhaps a school gymnasium or cafeteria). Play some gentle background music. Then have your class follow these instructions without talking:

Shape: *Make your body into a rounded shape. Then try straight, crooked, angular, open, closed, balanced, and unbalanced shapes.*

Level: *Make low, medium, and high shapes with your body. Strike several different poses for each level. Try combining different levels and shapes.*

Focus: *Use your body to direct the focus of a viewer in different directions. Try to make the eyes of an audience move up, down, sideways, forward, or into your center.*

Pathways: *Your body can move in straight or curved lines, in zigzags, back and forth, and up or down. Try moving in these different ways. Then pick a shape such as a square, a spiral, or a star and follow the outline of that shape with your body as if you were following a map.*

Ask for volunteers to try combining all of these elements into one series of movements. For example, one person might move with a twisted, low shape, directing focus toward the left while moving in a straight line to the right. Another person might make a straight shape at a high level, direct focus downward, and move in circles.

After you've explored different uses of space, try exploring the *how* of dance—energy. Energy has to do with the quality, exertion, and force of movements. It might include elements of speed and time, but you can focus energy in other ways, as well.

Exertion: *Move the body with powerful or delicate motions. Try making motions that are tight or loose, free or bound, smooth or sharp, wild or subdued.*

Emotion: *Try starting with a feeling or an abstract idea and searching for a movement to express it. Consider words like* love, hate, innocence, judgment, poetry, honor, gloom, *then try to strike poses or find movements to represent these words. Notice not just the pose or movement but the energy used to reach that shape.*

Again, practice these ways of moving for a few minutes, and then combine space and energy to create specific moods or impressions. You might try giving a few volunteers a situation and having them combine these elements to portray that situation using only gestures. Good situations might include the moment just after a fight with a friend, the moment before going on stage, a time you were embarrassed, or a time you fell in love with someone you didn't know well.

Writing Through Space and Energy

Obviously, the way people move is important for writers who want to show how characters feel without telling readers too much boring information. You can create endless scenarios, apply the elements of movement listed above to them, and then write scenes in which the way characters move is as important as what they say.

Writing also uses space and energy. The shape of a poem on the page makes a difference in how it's read. Some poems are percussive and sharp, while other seem to flow with smooth, soft energy.

Try suggesting the following approaches to your students:

Write the same poem twice—first in a long, thin shape, and then in a wide or meandering shape. An alternate possibility would be to re-line an old poem with a brand new shape. How does this change the meaning? [Along with this assignment, you can show students poems in different shapes. Look at poems by Lawrence Ferlinghetti, e.e. cummings, and George Herbert to see interesting shapes.]

Write a poem or story in which the main focus gradually changes during the course of the work. Use movement to change the focus away from or to one character or object. [An interesting poem to use in conjunction with this assignment is Margaret Atwood's "This Is a Photograph of Me," in which the speaker gradually directs attention away from the most noticeable objects in a certain scene and toward herself.]

Make a list of words involving movement. Using this list, write a piece that explores a particular pathway—spiral, zig-zagged, or curved. Let the action of the piece unfold through movement in imitation of whatever pathway you choose. [A journey of some sort would make a good subject.]

In the following poem, the speaker describes energy and shapes, and also uses focus to shift the center of the poem from the actual performers to an audience member:

The Dancer

Elizabeth watches them dance,
the ballet is unreal to her.
She tells her mother that the people
look like paintings or dolls,
they are too beautiful to be real.

She pulls her raven hair into a dancer's bun,
shapes her arms above her head,
and imagines a strong partner lifting her into the air.
Her older sister is the sugar plum fairy.
Elizabeth watches her stretch her long legs
before she begins to dance,
watches her feet move quickly over the floor.
She watches pirouette after pirouette,
then finally returns
to her room.

She pretends she is in center stage.
She turns and leaps,
then grows still to receive cheers from the audience.
She imagines her body as beautiful as a swan's
on long legs lowering to take a bow.
She closes her eyes
and hums the theme from the Nutcracker,
all the while spinning her wheelchair
round and round.

-Kristen Robertson, 9th grade

Follow-up Activities

1. What other physical activities do your students engage in using different types of energy? Have them write poems exploring an activity other than dance through the description of space and energy. Some good topics might be sports, fights, games, and conversations.

2. Have your students find a partner and practice moving in pairs. Partners can mirror one another's movements, direct each other, and

interpret an emotion through movement while the other person guesses what emotion that is. Then have your class write with their partners, choosing a common subject or set of movements for each person to include in a poem or story.

STAGES, SETS, AND COSTUMES .

Actors, directors, writers, and set and costume designers work together to create an atmosphere that makes a play believable. The process is a lot like that of a painter setting a scene. A theater company can move people or objects around, change backgrounds, dress actors, or make any other changes to the physical appearance of the stage and actors in order to help the audience enjoy the production. Writers, who sometimes use backdrops larger than those of any theater or movie set, need to think about how to create a believable atmosphere and setting as much as any actor, director, or designer.

Stage Directions

Staging (sometimes called *blocking*) begins with the writer. If you look back at the unit in this chapter on dialogue, you'll see one example of how a writer might put stage directions in the script by placing them between parentheses. You can find similar stage directions in any play you read.

Directors and actors interpret these stage directions to fit the needs, limitations, and interpretation of the whole production. It's a collaborative effort in which the writer offers an initial idea but (most of the time) agrees to accept a certain application of that idea.

Some writers, especially those who lived centuries ago such as Shakespeare or the Greek dramatists, leave most stage directions out. Others, including contemporary playwrights, tend to include extensive stage directions in the script. Either method might work to both the disadvantage and the advantage of a director or an actor; the first requires more creativity, while the latter might stifle new ideas.

Have your students look through several different plays, including a Shakespearian drama, a Greek tragedy like *Oedipus* or *Antigone,* and some more recent works such as plays by Tom Stoppard, Beth Henley, or Brian Friel. From each of these works, your students should pull a few stage directions and write them down on a slip of paper. Encourage them to

include both short, direct instructions and also elaborate and complicated directions.

Have one student draw a slip at random and choose the number of
people he or she needs to perform the scene. Give the ensemble a few
minutes to prepare (if you want, have several ensembles prepare at once),
and then watch the performance of the scene. When it's over, ask the
group to read its stage directions out loud.

Ask the class for observations and comments on the interpretation of
the directions. What choices were made? Were they effective? What other
interpretations might work with this set of directions? How do the stage
directions affect the emotional or thematic content of the scene?

Set Design

You can make backdrops for sets using either a single sheet of poster
board, a three-panel cardboard set, or a diorama made from a shoe box or
other cardboard carton. Supply your students with art supplies such as
markers, glue, scissors, and construction paper, and ask them to create a
miniature backdrop for their own works. A group of students working
together might create several backdrops for different scenes in the same
work. Tell the students they can include details that are not in the work,
although every detail that is in the work must also be included.

Display the results and discuss the process. How were decisions made?
What difficulties arose and how were they overcome? What details seemed
important that weren't in the original plan?

Sound Effects

Have each student or group of students take original works and add
sound effects to them. One student should read the work aloud while
others add the sound. If you like, allow the use of instruments, found
objects, or recorded sounds as part of this process. When the presenta-
tions of these works are finished, talk about the results just as you did
with set design. What worked well? What details emerged that weren't in
the original work?

Costumes

You can add costumes to figures in your set design, or you can have your
students dress up in order to read. The former is probably easier. Another
way to explore costume and makeup design is to use a blank face or the
outline of a body and color clothing and features onto it. Have your

students try a few different designs for their characters. You can also look through magazines and find the appropriate clothing to cut and paste onto a figure. Again, look for details that weren't in the original but that seem necessary in this format.

Any of these activities can also be used to re-create a work in a new setting, atmosphere, or period of time. They can also be applied to abstract pieces of writing, with more abstract artistic results.

The important point of these exercises for writing students is that they offer an opportunity to see what kinds of details and description are important to an audience that might not immediately spring to mind for a writer. Have your students make careful observations about the results of these activities, and then give them some of these ideas:

Write a piece that gives physical directions or instructions. Tell the reader how to move, speak, or feel.

Write a piece in which the location and position of characters is important. You might wish to "block" the piece in your mind before you start writing. Include descriptions of where characters stand, where they look, and how they move.

Write about a time when you changed your surroundings in order to change the way you or someone else thought, felt, or acted.

Write about a time when clothing was important to you. This might be the story of a specific article of clothing or of a time when an article of clothing or an outfit changed how someone felt or acted.

Directions and advice are often as important to the person giving them as they are to the recipient. If I were to give directions to the bookstore and restaurant owned by my relatives in Horse Cave, Kentucky, I could simply draw a road map. But that wouldn't impart the tastes, emotions, or excitement I feel whenever I make that trip. To do that, I'd have to tell someone about smelling the honeysuckle in early summer, watching for magnolia blossoms on the trees, ignoring the sticky, damp feel of clothing in the hottest weather in July, and tasting the pie at the restaurant. Those directions are every bit as important as turning left or right at each intersection. Here's a poem in which the speaker offers directions for living a single day. Notice the repetition of the second line at the end of the poem—just as the Earth moves in a circle each day "inch by inch," the poem also comes full circle.

How To Reach Twilight

Start at dawn.
Notice the sky, always notice the sky.
Sip coffee on the front porch
and watch the dog play in the yard.
Relish the chill dew under your feet
when you walk out to the curb for the paper.
Go to work, smiling on the way.
Hug someone when you get there.
Think of birds, and of someone you miss.
Purge a bitter memory or two.
Work long, make your day long,
make your mirth last.
Go home.
Sing to the indigo, melon clouds,
sing to your cat
(or your neighbor if you haven't got a cat).
Tell your friend about early laughter
and, as the sun, inch by inch,
mile by mile,
smiles on you and
moves to the other side of the planet,
notice the sky.

-Melanie Isom, 11th grade

Follow-up Activities

1. Go back and block some student poems or stories, even those they wrote just for this assignment. Is there any instruction or movement lacking in the poem or story that ought to be included, or that would make the result more entertaining, understandable, or interesting?

2. Find a scene from Shakespeare and have your students write detailed stage directions for it. Compare this to a screenplay of a recent movie

made of one of the plays (you can find these in most bookstores). How can the scene have different meanings according to the staging? Try writing your stage directions as a poem in and of themselves.

3. Sketch or create sets and costumes for works of literature or historical periods your students are studying. Then write pieces based on those works or just on the sets themselves. Be sure they include lots of interesting physical details, both in the sets and the written works.

HISTORICAL DRAMA

For any writer, it's both challenging and exciting to create a piece set against the background of another time. It's not easy for actors, either. Finding a personal, emotional link to a character who lived hundreds of years ago is a challenge whether you're creating that character from scratch or acting through dialogue that's already been written. There must be consideration on the part of both writers and actors for the thematic content and relevance of the work. How does it relate to life today? How can the audience access the lessons or issues in this work? Why is this story important?

Addressing all of these concerns has to be a mutual effort between the writer whose words are to be spoken and those who are speaking the lines. As you read or write material set in a time earlier than your own, remember that the most important part of your job as a writer, an actor, or an audience member is always to find the common links and lessons that cross historical boundaries through personal, emotional creativity.

Exploring Historical Subjects

Start by choosing the period or periods of history your students will explore. You might want to collaborate with a history teacher, an art or a music teacher, or even a science teacher to find a period of history in which interesting events, discoveries, or progressive moments existed. Your students might, for instance, each choose the life of a different artist to explore. You might have your whole class write about the same period, or different individuals or groups choose different periods.

Once your students have chosen a time to write about, have them do some research. They might go to the library and take notes, use the Internet, check encyclopedias, or conduct interviews with people who were alive at the time (grandparents make great resources). Once your students have some notes, put them in groups and have them make a visual collage, poster, or model that has to do with the stories of the historical period. Encourage creativity—characters, events, emotions, and themes all have a place in this sort of project. Your students can use magazine photos, construction paper, or any other materials that seem relevant to create these posters. Have the groups share the results with the class and then display them.

Next, have the same groups put together a two- or three-minute skit or scene that reflects one story from the period you're working with. Review the elements of acting *and* of writing they'll have to deal with. How should the characters speak? How should they look? What interesting actions or props should be included? What should the set look like? Does the event or story of the scene have a meaning particular to the time, or is the theme universal?

Allow your students to perform these scenes, and after each one discuss how a writer or an actor might want to change it or what they might want to keep the same. When your students are ready to write, give them this suggestion:

Find one character or story from your collage or scene. Think about the customs, speech, actions, mannerisms, appearance, and motivation of the character or characters. Write a poem or story in the voice of a historical person, trying to be true to history and yet to appeal to an audience of today.

I've found that it helps if there's a personal connection to the subject matter to begin with. In Tennessee, where I worked with African American students, I had them explore the periods of slavery, civil rights, or the rise of blues music. In other parts of the country you might have students explore the history of Native Americans, European immigrants, or frontier expansionists, just to name a few possibilities.

Here, for instance is a passage written by a student who looked to the injustices faced by her own ancestors and found a particular historical event that offered inspiration:

Through the Anger of Ethel Rosenburg

Do not cry for me,
for I speak to you in anger,

not behind tears.

Do not surrender in the face of death.
Yes, they will kill Julius and me,
but as I await my death tomorrow
my head remains high.
I will die with dignity.

Do not scream as you search for justice
among the entanglement of hate.
The big-time politicians who testified against us
blame another fault on us Jews.
Lies slid out of their mouths.
They spit swastikas at us.

"Russian spies;" they accused
that we shared the most valuable secret;
the formula for death.

But they had only looked at our faces,
our noses.
We are Jews.
We are only Jews to them.

-Rachel Bloomekatz, 10th grade

Not all stories and poems written about historical episodes need to be melancholy or despondent, but they often end up that way. That's probably because the most horrible events in history are those that stay with us the longest. Remind your students that they can write about historical successes and achievements as well as tragedies.

Follow-up Activities

1. Assign your students to write stories in first person that re-create the voice of a minor character from a historical drama. Fill in the gaps about what happens in between the scenes in which that character is actually on stage. For an example of this approach, look at Tom Stoppard's play *Rosencrantz and Guildenstern Are Dead.*

2. Have your students collect photographs and other memorabilia of their own family history from the time before they were born. Then have them write monologues in the voice of one of their own ancestors.

3. Have students rewrite a scene from a historical drama, giving it a contemporary setting without changing the theme or plot. These pieces can be written as a scene in a play or as a poem or story.

FILM AND TELEVISION

Film is perhaps the most multimedia form of art. Drama, music, visual arts, and even dance all contribute to most thirty-second television commercials. Feature-length movies use these elements even more. A movie director has to consider just about every element of the artistic process listed in this book. That's one reason the following assignments involving film can be valuable for your writing class; they force your students to think about the entire artistic process a frame at a time.

What can you do with film that you can't do with the other arts? Maybe nothing. There's no way to quantify the effectiveness of any single art form. Film doesn't necessarily provide deeper emotional resonance or educate us more than the other arts. Nonetheless, there's certainly something magical about the moving image. To be able to re-create the world so closely, but to change it at the same time, is a powerful tool for artists seeking to communicate meaning and emotion. Film, like writing, can be informative, entertaining, artistic, provocative, profane. Film makers have been learning from writers and other artists for an entire century. There's no reason we shouldn't be able to learn from them as well.

Discussing Film

You'll have no trouble getting a discussion about movies going with your students. Getting them to agree on what makes a good movie is a different matter. Try brainstorming a list of characteristics of movies or television shows your students like to watch. Don't judge any answers to begin with; just add anything that any student says to the list. Then, once you've come up with all of the elements of film that your class likes, see if you can categorize the responses. Which have only to do with entertainment? Which have to do with education? Which have to do with artistry?

Some of the responses may cross these categories. Pay close attention to those, for they're probably characteristics that film shares with writing, like story development, interesting characters, and good dialogue.

Once you've discussed the list, ask each student to write a paragraph or so about what makes a good film. Leave the interpretation of "good" up to the student. Have a few students read their responses out loud and discuss the answers.

Writing from Film

Life is not lived in isolated moments, nor in capsulized events. All of our experiences and emotions exist in the context of who we have become over an entire lifetime. Film, like long works of fiction, allows us to capture some sense of the continuity of life.

Have your students write about the process of making movies, and have them write about the characters or scenery they see in movies. My favorite writing assignment originating with film, however, comes from thinking about the way film is put together: in frames.

Any piece of film is actually made up of lots of still images seen one after another. One benefit of film is that the frames don't have to be consecutive. You rarely, in fact, see more than a few minutes of film shot continuously. Editors cut and splice scenes and even lines to make the product more interesting. Even videotape, which is not made up of frames, is used to connect individual scenes and is edited in the same way. Writers do the same thing; we pick and choose our moments carefully for best effect.

Have your students write poems or stories in frames, including small events from different periods of their lives in order to achieve a large story or theme. The events in each "frame" might be separated by days, weeks, or even years. What's more, each frame ought to be constructed with many elements in mind—the visual effect, sounds, movement, character development, and emotions.

Here's part of a long series of scenes by one student who used this technique to recall details of her life as she grew and matured:

Slides of Childhood

I.
You're making me Kool-Aid
and telling me a poem

that's one of your favorites.
You drop ice cubes in the purple liquid
and ask me if it's sweet enough.
I share some with my flowers,
and ask you to tell me a story.
"Once upon a time, there was a beautiful girl . . ."

II.
We're watching the Ronald Reagan show,
and you don't feel well.
I say, "Go to bed, I can tuck myself in tonight."
You lie down in pink satin PJ's and tell me you love me.
I turn out the light.

III.
At Uncle Lonnie's, Aunt Betty tries to keep me
from asking questions.
But I want to know why Mama is in the hospital.
Where's Mama? Where's Uncle Lonnie?
I surrender and lie down in the guest room
to watch the stars dance.
I say a poem in my head and wish you were here
to tell me the lines I can't remember.

IV.
I sit with Mama and Ned,
much too dressed up.
I should be comfortable, like you always are.
I wonder if there are books in heaven.

V.
Years pass.
I get older, write more, and listen to the muses
you told me about so long ago.
Sometimes they whisper of you,
or maybe it's just you whispering.

-Kristen Robertson, 10th grade

Follow-up Activities

1. Ask your students to create "commercials" for products that are abstract, like love, peace, anger, or revenge. Begin these as artistic projects, and then have them write serious pieces that try to sell the reader on an emotion or idea through the use of physical details and interesting language.

2. Ask each of your students to name three favorite movies. Then have them write scenes (in story, poem, or play form) in which a similar situation occurs but in which the plot takes a different path. The characters need not be exactly the same; in fact, it will probably be more interesting to set the scene with different characters in a different time, place, or context.

Chapter Four

Between the Lines

F O L K   A R T   A N D   C R A F T

*T*his final chapter includes the writing assignments and art forms that don't fit neatly under the general categories of visual art, music, or performance. There's no good label for these exercises. They include artistic activities that are sometimes called primitive or simple, but it's easy to find examples of any of these art forms that reflect a high level of skill and concern on the part of the artists. Even the terms "folk art" and "craft" don't really do these activities justice; these terms may also imply a level of simplicity that the arts included here may rise above. All of these activities share one thing in common with other art forms, including creative writing. They involve the expression of original thought and feeling in an aesthetic form.

As you read through the activities in this chapter, ask yourself if there's a difference between these forms of art and others with which you're familiar. What's the same or different about the process of creating a quilt and the process of creating an opera? How does drawing a comic book differ from painting on a canvas?

Q U I L T S

I'm not the only person with a quilt that reminds me of my family stories. In my case, the quilt on my bed reminds me of my great-aunt, Virgie Edwards, who owned a farm in Kentucky and died when she was over a hundred years old. Even if you don't own an old quilt, you've probably seen them in other people's homes, in stores, or even in museums. The stories they suggest have value for your students because they offer a tangible link to times, places, and people.

Traditional quilts from all over America share certain aspects. They're almost always made with a repeating geometric pattern, often constructed from small squares of cloth. They tend to be about the same size—roughly the size of a bedspread—although this has changed as quilts have become more decorative. They also rely on repetition of color as well as shape.

The result is often abstract and compelling. In fact, some critics have called quilts America's earliest form of abstract art.

Holding a Bee

You may have students in your class who have made quilts themselves; if so, you might ask them for help on this activity. You might also go to the library and check out a couple of books on quilts with pictures; look particularly for any that explain the significance of certain patterns.

Hold a "quilting bee" with your students. Divide the class into groups small enough to share materials but large enough to have a conversation while they work. Give each group scissors, construction paper, glue, and a large piece of white poster board. Then have them make posters of quilts.

Before they begin, the group should pick a pattern. The pattern might imitate a quilt they've seen, be an original abstract design, or be a design that contains a picture or the school initials. Allow your students some freedom in choosing their designs, and also allow them some freedom in choosing how to collaborate. Some groups may have one person cutting, another gluing, and another tracing the outlines of blocks, while other groups may allow everyone to work on each part.

The posters can be made using any shapes, but a traditional quilt form would be to cut squares about three inches on each side. Remind the students to think about patterns of color as well as shape.

When the posters are finished, have each group share its product and talk for a minute about the process. Then ask the students what sort of conversations they had with one another as they were working. Did they discuss the process itself for the most part, or did they talk about school, friends, and general gossip? Ask them what kinds of conversation they think might have taken place at quilting bees fifty, one hundred, or two hundred years ago.

Display the posters on a wall or table for everyone to see.

Writing Quilts

Before you do any writing, be sure to discuss the different possible methods of collaboration and how each made the students feel. The simplest approach for writing after this activity is to draw upon the ideas that the activity itself inspires. Ask your students to consider the following possibilities and to write about one:

Remember a quilt from your childhood. Who made it? What stories surrounded it or the person who made it?

What do the patterns in the quilt you made (or in someone else's quilt) remind you of? Are they metaphors? Are they representations of real objects?

If these ideas or others that arose during the process of making the quilts spark a poem or story, give your students the time to explore their memories in writing. Because some communities of students will be more likely to have owned handmade quilts as children, you might encourage your students to be imaginative and to put themselves in other situations and contexts in order to write this assignment.

When I was five years old my grandmother gave me a quilt for my birthday. I didn't *want* it—dolls and books were more my style—but I wrote a thank-you note and smiled dutifully. I slept under my quilt every night and eventually became attached to it. Still a little girl, I read under it with a flashlight until I became unconscious with exhaustion.

Now, in my teens—my poetic stage—I sit on it and pour my heart out to the always-forgiving paper. I look at it every now and then that there is a stitch for everyone in the world. Some tiny and precise; some big, loose, and careless. I found *my* stitch a while ago and colored it so I could find it. I look at it and decide that the intelligent-looking stitch on my right is my future husband, the one on my left my mother, and the ones stemming from my stitch are my children.

Each square is a different country, I decided; navy and white stripes for Canada, yellow with black paw prints for Africa, lush and brightly colored for Brazil. My stitch is in a white square—my race and destiny are undefined and I can fill in that ominous space any way I want—with patches of royal blue for success; maroon for love; and maybe a color no one has seen before.

-Rachel Dart, 8th grade

Follow-up Activities

1. Find a book about quilts with lots of pictures in it at your library or at a bookstore. Have your students choose quilts with interesting patterns or designs and write about them. What is the significance of the pattern? Who might have designed it? You might notice that many traditional patterns have interesting names—*The Fox and Geese, Hearts and Gizzards, Pandora's Box, The Tree of Paradise*—that would make good titles.

2. Quilts aren't the only kind of art to use pattern as a motif. One of the earliest uses of repeating designs can be seen in mosaics. Greek and Roman tile mosaics make interesting starters for fast-writes. Discuss the use of patterns in the mosaics as compared to patterns in quilts. How do the times, materials, and functions of the two cause them to differ? In what ways are they similar?

MASKS

I often start a lesson on masks by asking for a show of hands by everyone in the room wearing makeup. In high school classes, a few girls always have on some blush, lipstick, or eyeliner. Occasionally a boy does, too (some schools are more diverse than others). I ask everyone whose hand is raised what kind of makeup she's wearing and why.

The most common answer is "to make myself look better." Other students might toss out statements like "I'm insecure," "I want to en-hance certain features," or "I think other people like me better this way."

We change our appearance for all sorts of reasons. Sometimes, like brides at weddings, we hide our faces altogether; sometimes we put on masks when we trick-or-treat, play sports, ride motorcycles, or work with dangerous materials. Ultimately, most of our reasons for wearing various types of masks fall into four categories: protection, deception, making ourselves attractive, and traditional ceremony. It's easy to see any of these four purposes in the masks of native cultures from around the world.

The purpose of masks is to convey concepts and feelings, and the tool they use to do so is the artistic exaggeration of human features. Parts of faces are enlarged, reduced, or distorted to create the *impression* of a common experience or idea. Sometimes physical traits from animals are included in order to suggest the symbolic traits they represent. Sometimes the masks aren't meant to be worn at all; they're simply re-creations of a human semblance, an artistic statement.

You won't have any trouble getting students to make masks that convey interesting ideas; every mask does. Writing from masks offers a chance to put those ideas into words.

Mask Making

Before you begin, brainstorm a list of animals with your students, and beside each item write an attribute or symbolic idea that you identify with that animal. You might even research the beliefs of other cultures to find out what qualities different people have associated with those creatures.

Snakes are thought to be evil, coyotes tricky, rabbits speedy and fertile, turtles slow. Other cultures, however, may think of these animals differently. Some Native Americans believe that the turtle symbolizes Mother Earth and protection, and Ancient Greeks believed that snakes aided in healing (they're wrapped around the physician's staff, the caduceus). In island nations, fish are often used as symbols of wealth and prosperity. In China, dragons represent power and royalty.

Your students don't have to use animal features or symbols on their masks, but it's nice for them to have the option. I also like to discuss how different characteristics of masks change their message. Size, orientation (raised or lowered faces, for instance), and materials can all change a mask. Features and expressions are especially important. Long, pointed noses make a face seem wicked, while fat, bulbous noses make it seem comical. Horns give a devilish or animal-like quality to a face. Grins, screams, and open mouths suggest different emotions. Small eyes sometimes seem wise, while large, open eyes might suggest innocence or fear. Once you've thought about some of these characteristics as a class, you're ready to make the masks.

First, decide what materials you want to use. Paper bags, magic markers, and scissors are easy to start with; just cut holes for the eyes and decorate the face. A slightly more complicated approach is to use construction paper and glue. If you cut a large oval out of the paper and cut a slit in each end about three inches long, you can then overlap the edges of the two slits and tape them to create a shallow bowl shape.

Another possibility is to make a flat mask out of paper or cardboard. This sort of mask might cover your whole face or just your eyes, as many costume party masks do. (You might want to attach a dowel or pencil to hold such a mask to your face.)

After your students have made the basic "face" of the mask, the next step is decoration. Remind your class at this stage that it's important to think about what message the mask is intended to send. The decoration of the face will play a major role in the idea or emotion the mask sends to others. For decoration, your students can use paper, ribbon, yarn, paint, crayons, beads, dry macaroni, or just about anything else that comes to mind.

When all of the masks are finished, ask a few students to share their creations and explain how and why they chose to make the masks as they did. Some students might say they made their masks as they did just because "it felt right" or "it seemed cool," and that's okay, but try to get them to explain those feelings with a little more detail. *Why* did it feel right? What about the mask makes it cool?

As with all writing, the poetry and prose that comes from this assignment should rely as much on physical detail and description as on abstract ideas. Here are some questions you might ask to start your students thinking:

What masks do you wear from day to day? How do your masks change in different situations and at different times?

What about the mask you just created suggests aspects of your own character? Are there physical aspects of the mask that you prefer to your own face? Are there those that you do not prefer?

What might you say to this mask if you could address it directly?

Have your students keep their masks in front of them (or on their faces) while they write. Tell them they should look at the mask as they put words on paper so that they'll remember to keep their work concrete and physical.

In the following poem, the mask becomes a face that the speaker attaches to someone else and also a shield for the speaker himself.

The Happy Child
(fish mask)

He came from the family we envy.
They lived in a small palace

On the posh side of town–
The neighborhood that posts its own
Ornate street signs of wrought-iron.
Between the castles they call homes
And the rippling waves of manicured lawns,
They paraded their wealth to passers-by
In formations of foreign cars.

We continued pushing for money
As he desperately reached out—
Struggling to escape the torment
His family hid
Behind the mask of prosperity
We glued on their faces.
We failed to see anything
Except the money
That served only as a catalyst
To the problems we didn't know we shared.
By escaping this life,
He let us see the bitter world—
Once shielded by plastic smiles
And the dollar signs in our eyes.

In his safer new world,
He sits in grimy, second-hand clothes
And wears a fresh smile,
Unnoticed on the streets
Of a metropolis
That will never remember his name.

-Austin Adkinson, 11th grade

Follow-up Activities

1. Have each student cut out a blank, white face from a flat sheet of
   paper. Distribute crayons or markers, and have the students color
   both sides of the face. On the front or outside of the mask, students
   should choose colors, symbols, and features that reflect their external
   selves, those faces they show to others or that others perceive. On the

back or inside, they should represent their internal selves, the private faces they show only to themselves or those close to them. Then ask them to write about the differences and similarities between the two sides. They might even want to try a conversation between the two parts of their own selves.

2.   As a class, create masks that represent different characters, perhaps taken from a novel, story, or play your students have read (or from a story by someone in the class). Read passages of the work aloud while wearing the masks. Then write pieces from the point of view of individual characters in that work, or responses to those characters.

CARTOONS AND COMICS

Asking students to illustrate their own poems and stories is a fairly simple and common exercise for teachers. It's valuable for the same reasons that writing about art is valuable—it places creative writing in a physical context and forces students to think about visual imagery.

Creating comic strips out of student writing works well for a couple of reasons. For one thing, it's fun. Students don't have to worry about being "bad at art" when they're drawing comics, since comic strip pictures can be simple or "primitive." What's more, comics argue against abstractions and wordiness more clearly than any teacher can.

Creating Comic Strips

It doesn't take much introduction or discussion to get students working on their own comic strips. If you like, bring to class the comics section of your daily or Sunday paper and look at the techniques artists use. Notice the size, number, and shape of panels; speech and thought balloons; and methods of drawing. Also, ask some of your students to bring in comic books they've read.

Before your students create comics of their own, they might want to plan a little. Here are some steps you can tell them to follow.

Choose a poem or story to illustrate. This can be a work you've written earlier, one you write especially for this purpose, or even one by someone else in the class or a published poet or author. Divide the work into phrases for inclusion in the comic strip. Each phrase will be written and illustrated in a separate panel.

Once students have broken the piece into phrases, there are two ways to proceed.

1. They may wish to draw the comic strip one panel at a time. Have them decide on the size and shape of the first panel (round, square, rectangular), draw the panel and write in the words of the poem, and illustrate them. You might wish to make copies of several panels for the class to share.

2. They might want to draw all of the panels first, and then insert the text and pictures. The advantage of this method is they won't run out of space on the page toward the end of the comic strip. If your students wish to create more sophisticated comic strips, suggest that they first create a storyboard by making preliminary sketches of the entire strip. This rough draft will allow them to revise and rethink before they commit themselves to more intricate, detailed work.

Students can write the text at the top or bottom of the panel, in a speech or thought balloon, or in any other way they can think of. Encourage them to be creative and try different types of panels, pictures, and lettering, as well as color for the drawings and background.

When you finish creating comics, either display them on the wall of your classroom, or distribute them to other students, parents, and teachers. You may choose to sell the comics individually for a few cents each, give them as gifts, or bind them together in a printed book for distribution.

Follow-up Activities

1. Choose a well-known comic like *Peanuts* or *Batman.* Have your students write poems or monologues from the point of view of one of the characters (especially characters other than the main character). Include descriptions of what's going on outside, before, or after the frames of the comic.

2. Have your students draw pictures in a comic format first, and then trade papers with other students. The second student to get a paper should write a poem or story to fit the pictures. Don't allow any communication between the artist and writer until both have finished.

GRAFFITI AND PICTOGRAPHS

Most of us can find forms of graffiti without looking very hard—on water towers, in public bathrooms, on bridges, or on walls. The messages people leave in such places range from simple names to elaborate poems, jokes, and even letters. Ask your students to recall some of the interesting comments or drawings they've seen (you might even make it an assignment for them to go look at more). Some of the responses might surprise you. We tend to forget graffiti pretty easily, but sometimes a particularly witty or interesting remark sticks in our minds. That's the power of words and images that your students can see and use in this unit.

Native American Pictographs
Many primitive cultures have left carvings, cave paintings, or other forms of art behind even after other traces of their presence have vanished. Frequently, the main subjects of these portrayals are animals and the way humans interact with them. On this continent, Native American tribes relied on animals for food, clothing, and spiritual guidance. It's not surprising that they should show up in their art.

Was it an act of vandalism or of artistic expression for Native Americans to carve pictures of animals into rock faces? The answer, perhaps, lies in the purpose of the drawings. Unlike some graffiti that are only intended to debase or to offend, Native American drawings were created for other reasons. Animals, for many tribes, symbolized a spiritual connection to the world. By drawing pictures of them, along with pictures of other natural objects such as plants, flowers, or the sun and moon, men and women personalized the world around them and formed a tangible connection to their surroundings.

It's the same thing we do as writers. Our poems and stories rely on physical detail and description because such details connect to and teach us about our world. Drawing or carving an animal or plant may be a more basic expression of that connection, but the urge to create comes from the same source.

Of course, Native Americans left drawings on more than just walls; they also decorated possessions such as clay pots, baskets, weapons, and clothing. Often animals were carved as totems out of rock, wood, or bone, and could then be carried or worn to provide guidance and protection.

You can find lots of these pictographs reproduced in clip-art books easily found in libraries and bookstores. I've included some here, but they are only a small sample of the many depictions of animals and other natural objects that are readily available. Here are a few drawings you might use:

Have your students choose one design or animal they feel closely connected to for some reason. In choosing, they might want to consider the traits of the animal and how we think of it. Butterflies, for instance, have transformed themselves; dogs are considered loyal; beavers are builders.

Sometimes I also read a few Native American myths and legends, or even some contemporary poetry, to a class before I have them choose an animal. First of all, this helps students choose, since these stories frequently feature characters such as Coyote (the trickster) or Mole, who lives underground because he has to hide from a magician. Second, many Native American myths attempt to explain why things happen or how they came to be, which is really just another attempt (like the drawings) to make sense of the world around us.

After your students choose their animals, give them all a four-inch square of poster board and have them draw their animal or symbol on it using color magic markers. While they're drawing, you might want to read them some more stories or poems, or play some Native American music. Once the drawings are finished, each student will have an animal totem. The totems are often both visually striking and personally relevant.

If you wish, you can also simulate rock carvings by having all of your students draw their totems on one large piece of paper taped to the wall. Whether you make individual totems or a combined decoration, ask your students to carry a small totem or design with them for a while. When they make decisions, speak, or act, they should consider whether they're demonstrating qualities like those of their animals.

When you're ready to write, tell your students they can address the totem animal directly, ask for its advice, and even tell it their secrets. Or they might choose to write about the connection they feel to the animal. Either way, ask them to include a physical description of the animal or of themselves, and to be physical in the way they write about their connections to the totem.

In the following poem about an otter, Melissa Warren points out ways in which she is the same as and different from her totem animal, and ends by wishing she could change:

Playing Otter

Tumbling in a bed
of green strings,
fur slicked with saltwater,
the otter pauses
and lifts her moon-shaped eyes
to mine.
This half-sized me
floats with the surf off Seattle coast,
dipping and diving
to the rhythm of crabs
scattering over sun-roasted sand.

While I,
on my city block,
hear her music only
through the conch
on my bathroom sink
as I press it over my ear.

I would have me be more like her,
cracking abalones on my belly
as the tide carries me
through warm water,
and all the day smiling
with pair upon pair
of moon-shaped eyes.

-Melissa Warren, 11th grade

Follow-up Activities

1. Graffiti are a great source for found poems. Have your students record real words and messages they find around your school or neighborhood, and then write poems using the phrases they've found. Ask them to imagine who might have left the messages and why.

2. Write myths based on Native American folklore and legend. First, brainstorm a list of natural occurrences to explain—begin each phrase with "why" or "how." Some examples might include "why it rains," "how the zebra got its stripes," or "why the sun returns each morning." Then, have your students pick one item from the list and write a myth in the form of a story or poem.

3. Totem poles were created by some Native American tribes on the Pacific coast. Usually, each totem on the pole symbolized one family unit. You might divide your students into groups and have each group contribute to a totem pole made from construction paper masks and designs attached in a column on the wall. Then have them write about the process of creating the totem, bonding with a group, or how their totem interacts with the others.

POSTCARDS

You've probably spent time standing at a rack of postcards, trying to find one that's not too tacky but that shows where you are and what you're doing. Postcards are practical; they allow us to communicate without belaboring the conversation, and they let us share a small moment of an adventure with those we care about. But are they art?

I hope that by now you can see what I mean when I say that I consider art to exist as much in the process of creation as in the product. The act of creation contains the moment when abstract ideas are connected to tangible, physical acts—painting, moving, singing—and it's those ideas that writers want to express through their own form, words.

Postcards have the benefit of containing both visual art and words. The visual art, of course, might be a photograph, a drawing, or some other design. Often the photographs on postcards are dated, poorly framed, or silly, but they do express some meaning or sentiment. The words often include a description of the art on the front of the postcard, but there are also the words the sender adds. However terse or uninspired the message, it too expresses an idea or emotion.

In fact, if you think about it, a postcard is a fantastic way of blending art and writing. It connects the two in an immediate fashion, it offers a solid context and background for its subject matter, and it has a built-in audience (albeit a very small one). And postcards force the writer (and the artist) to express ideas in a brief space, which is often not a bad idea.

So yes, I think that postcards are art.

Before you try this assignment with your class, you might want to bring some postcards from various sites and parts of the world and look at them together. If none of your students have saved old postcards, you can probably find a few at a local antique store. Which is the funniest, silliest, oldest, most sentimental? Which has the most interesting or attractive artwork? What's the message of the card?

It's not a bad idea to include at least a few cards that have actually been mailed to you. Let your students read the messages aloud and discuss the content and form. Is this good writing? Do the messages carry the emotional force they were intended to bear, or do they fall flat because of brevity and a lack of originality?

You might even display some of these cards in your room. If nothing else, they'll bring to mind some interesting places beyond the walls of your school.

Group Postcards

Give each of your students a sheet of plain white paper to start this exercise. Ask them all to close their eyes and think of somewhere else in the world they'd like to be. It can be a specific place, like Bangkok, or a general destination, like the beach or in a mountain cabin.

If you like, ask your students to think of their lives as a journey, with a destination at the end and stops along the road. You can specify the point at which they should think of themselves—the present, the moment they graduate from high school, when they publish a book—or you can have them think of any stop along the road.

Have the students draw pictures as if illustrating postcards from the destination that they've thought of. The illustrations might contain one image or several, and might be abstract or concrete. Let them use markers or crayons.

When each student has one image, put them in small groups with poster-sized paper and markers. The job of the group is to create a single postcard that includes at least one aspect or item from each person's picture. Again, the illustrations can be as creative or as simple as the group wishes, but the students will have to be able to explain the image when they're done. If the group wants, it can include a small blurb on the back of the "postcard" describing the image on the front. Give your students some time to create their drawings, and then have each group share with the rest of the class. Display the posters on a wall or table.

Your requirements for the writing portion of this activity should include only two rules. First, the pieces should relate to the postcard drawing. Second, they should be *to* someone.

Here's an example of how to introduce this assignment:

Imagine that you're actually sending this postcard to someone. Who would you send it to? What would be important to tell them? What physical description would you use? What metaphors? Write a letter to that person in a poetic or narrative form.

When your students are ready, have them write stories or poems that are, in essence, letters to another person. They might emerge as letters to a particular person, to one's self, or to a time or an idea. One group created a postcard of a high school senior gazing at an old yearbook. Behind her hangs her graduation gown. Here's an example of a poem from that assignment:

A Postcard from the End of High School

Not to say the weather here isn't beautiful,
or that I'm not relaxing for the first time
in years,

but it's a little disconcerting,
a little strange, and I'm not sure you'd understand.

You, who stare ahead hopefully,
whose ribboned blonde hair
and braces speak of innocence.
Your T-shirt and thin cheeks
remind me of myself (but you're not me,
not who I am or who I've become,
you're just a part of something I was).

The natives aren't as friendly here
as I'd been told. Besides,
everything's just a little different:
the language, the customs, the taste of things.

Not to say I want to come home.
No, it's just that I wish I'd packed a little better.

-Sarah Joe, 11th grade

Follow-up Activities

1. Create actual poetry postcards for friends, family, or famous people. Take a poem and/or an illustration in black and white and photocopy it on card stock. Then cut the picture down to postcard size. Most copy centers can help you do this. You can also buy blank stamped postcards from the post office and paste a poem on one side, or you can buy a box of perforated blank postcards that you can run through a printer or photocopier.

2. Many letters serve a particular purpose—apologies, sympathy notes, love letters. Have your students write a poem that addresses a particular person in the form of one of these letters. Tell them to be specific and detailed, not to fall back on abstractions. You might go back to the exercise involving greeting cards in the introduction to the chapter on visual art before trying this exercise. You could also read "This Is Just to Say," by William Carlos Williams, as an example of an apology poem.

Conclusion

There are a lot of exercises in this book, but I hope that every teacher who uses them will be inspired to create more of his or her own. It's the lessons to which you feel personally drawn that you'll teach best and that will result in the most original writing by your students.

In thinking about this conclusion, I asked myself these questions: Where will I, as a teacher, go from here? What's the next step? Now that I've taught every lesson in this book (and I'll surely use them again, but not exclusively), what do I do next?

The answer is that I have to challenge myself to look for more ways to stimulate student learning (and my own). Here are some steps you can follow as you continue to look for new ways to teach writing in your classroom:

- *Design further assignments.* As I mentioned earlier, almost any interesting and thought-provoking activity can be turned into a writing assignment. The trick? Just look for the larger issue, the thematic connection, the emotion. This works whether you're looking at techniques involving the arts or at any other activity. It's impossible to cover every aspect of art in one book, so there are plenty of areas left to explore—architecture, engraving, wood carving, weaving, embroidery, and origami, just to name a few. The basic format of the assignments in this book includes a discussion, an activity, a model, and a writing prompt. Put together those elements for any area in which you're interested and your students will probably respond.

139

- *Design units of study.* This book deals with the connections between creative writing and the arts. There are connections between the other art forms themselves, and even connections between the arts and science, social studies, and other areas of study. Put together activities that might form a unit for a piece of literature or theme your students are studying. A unit on African or African American literature, for instance, might include lessons involving visual art, movies, African music, or mask making. A unit on Shakespeare might include listening to or watching Tchaikovsky's *Romeo and Juliet.* Other themes to explore might include mythology, women's literature and art, exploration and discovery, or legends and fairy tales. Find paintings, musical compositions, plays, dances, and other artistic creations that revolve around a single theme and tie them all together with writing assignments. It's an exciting way to teach, and an exciting way for students to learn.

- *Study the arts.* The arts aren't limited to the elements and techniques presented in this book. Each time you listen to the radio, watch a play, watch television, or look at a picture, ask yourself what methods are being used, what skills are being drawn upon, and how those methods and skills contribute to the overall message and entertainment value of the piece. Teach your students to think critically about the arts and to enjoy them at the same time. The value of such thought is that it not only makes for more thoughtful writers, it also makes for more thoughtful human beings.

- *Study the art of writing.* Just as you watch for techniques in the visual and performing arts, help your students learn to watch for techniques that writers use. Rhyme, meter, voice, tone, and subject matter are all elements that every writer considers when he or she creates a work. By reading carefully and paying attention to these elements, students learn to improve their own writing.

Write every day. Make things. Don't stop. Put art into everything you do. Enjoy and respect the process every bit as much as you enjoy and respect the product.

Appendix

A GUIDE TO RESOURCES ON
THE INTERNET

The Internet provides a comprehensive and inexpensive source for giving your students access to great museums, dance and theater companies, classical music information, and arts organizations. Often, students can find these works themselves. Below are just a few of the excellent sites available.

VISUAL ARTS

The Greatest Painters on the Web (http://Kultur-online.com/greatest). A site to view and buy reproductions of many famous works of art from Western painters.

Museums Around the World (http://www.comlab.ox.ac.uk/archive/other/museums/world.html). A connection to famous and interesting museums in many countries.

Art History Resources (http://witcombe.sbc.edu). This site provides links to galleries and research sources.

The Metropolitan Museum of Art (http://www.metmuseum.org), The Museum of Modern Art (http://www.moma.org), The Art Institute of Chicago (http://www.artic.edu), The Louvre (http://www.paris.org/Musees/Louvre). Connections to some of the world's great museums.

141

M U S I C

Classical Music on the Web U.S.A. (http://www.unc.edu/~baker/music.html). Also provides information on folk music and instruments, jazz, blues, etc.

Yahoo Music (http://www.yahoo.com/entertainment/music). A good resource for classical and popular music.

The Classical Music Pages (http://w3.rz-berlin.mpg.de/cmp). More classical music information.

D A N C E

The New York City Ballet (http://www.nycballet.com). With links to reference material, history, and general dance information.

O T H E R   A R T S   A N D   G E N E R A L   A R T S
I N F O R M A T I O N

The Kennedy Center's Artsedge (http://artsedge.kennedy-center.org/ae-ug.html). Arts information, including education and links to folk art sites.

World Wide Arts Resources (http://wwar.com). General arts information.